Licensing Digital Content

A Practical Guide for Librarians

LESLEY ELLEN HARRIS

AMERICAN LIBRARY ASSOCIATION
Chicago and London
2002

Cover by Tandem Design

Composition by ALA Editions in Electra and Univers typefaces using QuarkXPress 4.1 for the PC

Printed on 50-pound white offset, a pH-neutral stock, and bound in 10-point cover stock by McNaughton & Gunn

ISBN: 0-8389-0815-2

Printed in the United States of America

06 05 04 03 02   5 4 3 2 1

To Bennett and Ari

CONTENTS

ACKNOWLEDGMENTS

I would like to thank the numerous people who generously gave their time and shared their experience and knowledge in helping me write this book. They include Kenneth Crews, Rina Pantalony, Gail Dykstra, Ken Wasch, Jerremie Clyde, and Lisa Gobert.

My thanks to Tarshel Beards, who initially contacted me about writing this book, Patrick Hogan, the editorial director, and others, including Mary Huchting, at ALA Editions. I also thank my editor, Paul Mendelson.

And thank you to all the people who e-mailed me questions for inclusion in chapter 7, and to those who asked me questions during the numerous seminars I have taught on licensing, and who made me think about many of the issues discussed in this book.

INTRODUCTION

Do I need a written agreement when licensing digital content?
Who is authorized to use the content my library licenses?
What if the license offered to our library is nonnegotiable?
Is electronic archiving allowed under our license?

These are a sampling of the many questions that have arisen over the past four years in the seminars I have been leading on digital licensing for librarians and others. The same questions arise again and again. Librarians are frustrated by the lack of resources providing answers to these and other questions. This book has been written to set out the basics about digital licensing for librarians, and to discuss the questions and issues that arise when interpreting, negotiating, and entering into digital licenses. My hope is to inform you about legal rights and obligations in license agreements, how to negotiate the best license to meet your needs, and the variety of licensing arrangements which can be used. Chapter 7 of this book sets many specific questions I have been asked by librarians at seminars and by e-mail, with answers to help you through the licensing process.

Licensing content is a specialty that seemed to appear out of the blue and, for some libraries, now encompasses the full-time job of at least one librarian. And yet there are very few print resources on licensing digital content aimed at librarians. The purpose of this book is to help demystify the licensing process and to provide you with a clear understanding of licensing in the specific context of a library or resource center. It is intended for libraries of all sizes and types, including public, government, college and university, K–12, and special libraries.

Although the information in this book is provided from the perspective of a library, it should be helpful for publishers and other content owners who license their content to libraries, as it will educate them on the licensing process through a library's eyes. Other users of electronic databases and periodicals, such as archives, museums, governments, educational institutions, and corporations, should also find valuable information in this book when they are licensing digital resources for use in their institutions.

This book is meant as a practical guide; it does not set out a comprehensive review of this area of the law, which may encompass contract law, copyright law, and other areas. Nor should this book be relied upon as providing legal advice. Proper legal consultation should be obtained where necessary.

As a practical book, there are checklists and precedents provided in it or referred to. Use them by adapting them to fit your particular needs in your specific circumstances. Determine whether the clauses in the checklist are relevant to your situation. Keep in mind that a license agreement that works for one library may not fit the needs of another library. It may not even fit the needs of the same library in two different licensing situations for different digital content.

I began providing information in this area through a few conferences I attended at which I led a seminar on digital licensing. Shortly afterward, I began giving the same seminar through my own company, Copyrightlaws. com, and often in conjunction with various library and other associations, to audiences ranging from six to sixty persons. I presented this seminar, which I continue to teach today, throughout Canada and the United States, and in London. I get requests from around the world about presenting this seminar in other countries. The audiences remain steady, and in some cities where I teach the seminar repeatedly, the audiences have grown. I have also been busy writing articles on digital licensing for libraries in North American and international library publications, and in *The Copyright and New Media Law Newsletter: For Libraries, Archives and Museums*, which I also edit. Further, I have helped a number of clients determine their strategy in licensing digital content. These experiences have led me to write this book in order to provide a one-stop source for librarians to find information on licensing digital content.

While reading this book, keep in mind that digital technology is rapidly changing and so is the way we license works in the digital environment. As such, any discussions of relevant licensing terms and conditions should be carefully reviewed in light of the most up-to-date technological and legal developments, and in light of your own circumstances. For instance, a library licensing an electronic database would have different concerns than a library licensing a photograph for posting on its own Web site, or a library licensing a manuscript from its collection for use on someone else's Web site or intranet.

LAST WORD

My final introductory comment is to "have fun." Digital licensing is a fun area because it is new and requires creative solutions. When you work out a satisfactory agreement to both involved parties, it can be a very rewarding experience. Keep in mind that you will be contributing to what one day may evolve into an industry standard in the digital licensing world—a standard that we all strive for while trying to understand this complex and convoluted area of law.

I am always interested in hearing your suggestions about licensing. I may be reached at libraries@copyrightlaws.com.

NOTE TO CANADIAN
AND
OTHER NON–U.S. READERS

Because this book is published by the American Library Association, some readers may assume that it is intended solely for an American audience. Let's correct that misimpression.

Digital licensing by its very nature implies global or worldwide licensing. This could mean that the content owner is based in one country and the library in a different country. Or it may mean that both the content owner and the library are in the same country, but the patrons or end-users of the licensed content are temporarily or permanently based in a different country. There are many variations on these scenarios that could further illustrate the nature of global licensing.

This book is written from the perspective of global licensing. In some situations, there will be discussions of country-specific issues. For example, in the United States, certain institutions have specific requirements that must appear in all licenses. Another example is moral rights that exist to some extent in the United States, more so in Canada and the United Kingdom, and very strongly in European Union countries. Other discussions in this book deal with these global issues, such as the portions in chapter 2 on international copyright law, the parts in chapter 4 on authorized users and authorized sites, and the sections in chapter 5 on governing law.

No matter where your library is based, where the content owner is based, and where your patrons are accessing the licensed content, you will soon find that negotiating your digital licenses must take into account global issues.

QUICK-STARTER TIPS
FOR A SUCCESSFUL AGREEMENT

This book is full of tips to help you ensure your license agreements work for you. However, for those looking for a "crash course," the following are seven basic points you should always keep in mind when negotiating digital licenses.

1. *Avoid oral licenses.* Although not always mandatory, use written agreements. Your written license is a summary of the terms and conditions of use of the licensed content and will be used for interpretation purposes by you and others in your library throughout the duration of the license.

2. *Understand your obligations.* Before signing on the dotted line, make sure you understand and are comfortable with the obligations the license demands of you. Do not base your agreement on any oral representations. If you see a clause you do not like, but the other party tells you not to worry because it will never be enforced, get that clause removed. Make sure you can live up to any obligations in the agreement.

3. *Cover all issues.* Do not avoid inserting any relevant issues in the agreement because you think those issues might "scare off" the other party. It is best to put everything on the table at the beginning and to avoid disputes in the future.

4. *Avoid legal language.* Simple nonlegalistic language is the best approach. You want wording that is clear to the two parties signing the agreement, and to anyone who needs to interpret or apply that agreement later. Defining any ambiguous or new technical words can help with this.

5. *Use consistent words and terms.* Do not use "content" in one clause, "material" in another clause, and then "publication" in a third clause.

6. *Be creative, patient, and flexible.*

7. *Know when to walk away.*

When to License

A wise man hears one word and understands two.

—Yiddish proverb

The digital revolution has resulted in an important, and sometimes daunting, change in the way libraries procure, access, and store information available for use by their patrons. In the pre-Internet and pre-electronic days, libraries regularly purchased print copies of materials for their collections and patrons. Libraries owned physical copies of these materials. We are now witnessing a revolution in how information is acquired, stored, and accessed. With this revolution comes a new set of administrative and legal issues librarians must face, some say a Pandora's box. No longer are librarians solely concerned about copyright law issues like photocopying in their libraries, or whether showing a video might constitute a public performance. Librarians have become negotiators and interpreters of legal agreements which open the door to a wide variety of electronic content for their patrons. Licensing electronic content is now an expected part of collections management, especially as more and more collections budgets are dedicated to serials available only in a digital format. Many librarians are already involved with licensing electronic or digital information, and many others will become more involved in this process in the near future.

Licensing electronic content rather than physical ownership of print copies raises a whole series of issues not previously experienced by librarians. Unlike signing a purchase order for a new print book or print periodical, licensing digital information often involves negotiating a license agreement or contract with the owner of the digital content for use in your library. At the very least, it involves understanding and interpreting such agreements, whether they are negotiated by a consortium on your library's behalf, are nonnegotiable, or are individually negotiated by your library. But when does a library need a written license, and how does the process begin? What terms and conditions are in the best interests of the library? What do these terms and conditions mean?

WHEN DOES LICENSING COME INTO PLAY?

Licensing comes into play when you want to use electronic or digital content such as a database or periodical, or when someone wants to use such content owned by your library. It may begin with a telephone call, an e-mail, a postal mail letter (commonly referred to as "snail mail"), an order form, or when you are offered a written license agreement.

Consumer/Licensee

As a *consumer* of content, you need a license agreement whenever you "use" the content of others. For example, you want to use someone else's photograph on your Web site, or you want to access an online database or periodical. "Use" in this context includes many different concepts or rights that are set out in copyright laws and treaties. Among these rights are the right to reproduce or publish in digital or print form, transmit over the Internet, and perform the work in public. "Use" also refers to content that is protected by copyright and is not in the public domain.

As a library or consumer of copyright materials, you may be involved in a number of situations in which you need to license content. You may need to license:

- An online subscription to a journal or database
- Content compiled by an aggregator such as Lexis-Nexis
- An encyclopedia or other collections of content
- Financial information, stock market sources, and news feeds
- Computer software, CD-ROMs, and DVDs
- Preexisting content for use on your Web site or intranet (including text; graphic content, such as maps and photographs; music; and video)
- Web site content
- Intranet content

Generally, libraries see themselves as consumers or *licensees*, using the content of others. However, more libraries are licensing the content they own, and are therefore also *licensors*. This is especially true as e-commerce continues to grow and libraries become more involved in e-commerce and selling intellectual property online.[1]

Content Owner/Licensor

As a *content owner*, you require a license agreement whenever someone else "uses" your content. Content that a library might own includes photographs, slides, reports, manuscripts, and audiovisual works. As an owner of content, you may be involved in some of these possible scenarios:

> Licensing a handful of works to be used in association with works by other creators. For instance, licensing three photographs from your library's collection for use in a Web site with other photographs, text, animation, etc.

> Licensing content owned by your library that would constitute all of the works to appear in a new media product. For example, a library might license digital rights to its manuscript collection for use by a developer in a CD-ROM who would then create a CD-ROM of manuscripts in your library.

> Licensing works for "relicensing" purposes. For instance, you might license the rights to digitize your library's newsletter to one company, which will then relicense these rights to CD-ROM or DVD producers, Web site owners, corporations, and others.

The focus in this book is from the perspective of a library licensing the content of others. However, if you are licensing your own content, you will go through the same procedure as a user of content, and you may use the same licensing checklists as provided in chapters 4 and 5, although you will have to approach the issues from a different perspective in order to protect your library's interest as a content owner.

Other Agreements

There are other agreements you may need in the digital world, including the following:

- Web site terms and conditions of use
- Privacy policy/release

- Web site development agreement
- Chat room agreement
- Click-through or Webwrap agreement
- Linking agreement
- Domain name assignment agreement

Although these agreements may not per se be content licensing agreements, many of the clauses discussed in this book are helpful when entering into such agreements.

NEGOTIABLE AND NONNEGOTIABLE LICENSES

License agreements may be negotiable or nonnegotiable. A negotiable agreement is one where the parties to the agreement discuss and agree upon what terms and conditions should be included in the agreement. When licensing digital information for use in your library, you will be able to negotiate with the owner various terms and conditions in the agreement, such as price of the material and who may use that material.

A nonnegotiable agreement is one where the terms and conditions in the agreement are set forth by one party and must be accepted by the other party if he or she wants the goods or services supplied. For example, you may find a nonnegotiable agreement when purchasing software from your local computer store. A company like Microsoft sets out the terms and conditions of use of its software. If you want to purchase and use its software, generally you must accept the terms and conditions of its agreement. The same may be true when downloading software from the Internet, in which case you may agree by pressing the "I Agree" button on a Webwrap license. However, even licenses that appear to be nonnegotiable are often negotiable, and you should always contact the content owner should you need to discuss terms and conditions that make the license more workable for your circumstances. Chapter 6 deals with negotiation issues relating to license agreements.

UNDERSTANDING THE CONCEPT
OF ELECTRONIC MATERIALS

One of the major changes in acquiring electronic content, as opposed to print journals, is that in many circumstances, libraries now pay for content they never physically acquire. For instance, a library pays for an online journal that it may never see in a print form (other than perhaps printed from its own printer). What the library is paying for is *access* to that online journal, not physical ownership of something it can place on its bookshelves. In addition, the scope of that access or use of the online journal may be more limited than the use of the print journal. For instance, it is not necessary to obtain permission to browse through a print journal, but permission may be necessary to access online content.

Libraries are very concerned about having access to archives of digital content. Whereas a print book may be kept and accessed from a bookshelf indefinitely, access to digital content has a defined duration. This is further discussed in various parts of this book.

Further, although print publishers are concerned about their works being photocopied, electronic publishers are even more threatened since it is so quick, easy, and inexpensive to make a copy of an electronic work. Controlling and monitoring electronic works is therefore a much larger problem than in the print world. In this regard, technology such as encryption, password-protected access, watermarking, and the use of PDF files may be necessary to ensure authorized uses only.

In addition, the types of uses requested by libraries and their patrons are different with digital content than print materials. For instance, in the academic world, print course materials often include excerpts from articles. With electronic library reserves and course materials available online, it is becoming more commonplace for entire articles—and not just excerpts—to be posted as part of these electronic collections. Many publishers are not opposed to this, provided they are fairly compensated and there are some "controls" in place to protect against further or unauthorized copies being made.

FIVE KEY LICENSING CONCERNS

Given the relative newness of licensing content in a digital form, libraries and online publishers have a number of concerns and needs which should be taken into account in any discussions or negotiations of license agreements. Throughout the licensing process, both parties should keep in mind that the license they sign should be a "win-win" situation. Although at times it may seem like each party has opposite interests, they are both aiming toward the same goal—*fair access at a fair fee*. For a library, "fair" may mean use according to its needs. For a publisher, "fair" may mean controlled access for authorized uses. For both parties, "fair" would also relate to the fee being paid for the content.

The following are five key elements libraries should aim for when licensing digital works. These elements may act as basic underlying principles upon which a license may be based. Specific details based on these principles are discussed throughout this book.

1. Ease of access to the works being sought (that is, easy online retrieval/download)
2. "One-stop" transactions where no additional permission, payments, or clearances are required once the library has chosen and paid for the works requested
3. Clear definitions of what uses are permitted and what uses are not permitted, by whom and where
4. Access beyond the termination of the license agreement
5. Liability regarding the use of licensed content by researchers and the public. For instance, how far must a library go to ensure that a researcher is using an article from an electronic publisher according to the terms and conditions of the license agreement?

THE RELATIONSHIP BETWEEN PRINT AND ELECTRONIC SUBSCRIPTIONS

Some journals distinguish their print from their electronic publications in terms of subscriber access and fees. Others permit certain electronic access with a print subscription. As electronic publishing becomes more popular, many more journals will only publish electronically. At the current time, any of the following scenarios are possible:

Only print subscribers have access to electronic content
- the library may have to pay an additional fee for the e-content, or
- the e-content may be "free" and considered part of the print subscription

Print and electronic subscriptions are dealt with separately, i.e., whether or not the library has a print subscription, it pays the same price for the e-content as a library who only subscribes to the e-content

Library/institutional subscribers may access online content; individual subscribers may not (and may only have access to print journals)

Timing of online publications
- same time as print publications
- prior to print publication
- after print publication
- archives only

Access to electronic versions may be
- full access to all electronic content
- access to certain electronic content
- separate pricing for different content, i.e., paying separately for current works and works in archives

As more and more libraries begin to convert their print acquisitions to electronic acquisitions in order to save space in a physical library and allow for broader access for their patrons, publishers will likely respond by allowing electronic licenses to works in which the library does not have or is not required to have a print subscription. Again, this would be a way of meeting the goals of both the content owner and the library.

DIFFERENCES IN ELECTRONIC AND PRINT VERSIONS

Digital and print versions may not be identical. The digital version may not have the illustrations, photographs, diagrams, etc., that appear in the print version, and many digital versions are only text. Further, the digital version may only contain portions of the text from the print version. On the other hand, the digital version might be interactive, more easily searchable, and contain flash animations not found in the print version. A digital version created from a print version may contain errors, including spelling errors. This often happens when the digital version is scanned from the print version using optical character recognition.

Other considerations to take into account in acquiring either a print or electronic version of content is that often an otherwise expensive e-version may be significantly less expensive if you also have a print version. Also, some publishers require you to subscribe to the print version in order to be able to use or subscribe to the electronic version. These are things you may wish to inquire about prior to licensing digital content.

ARE THERE INDUSTRY STANDARDS IN LICENSES?

There is no industry standard for licensing content by libraries. Digital content and digital distribution are relatively new. Developments in this area are considered to be "first generation." Digital license agreements, in general, were initially a hybrid of computer software, book publishing, and film agreements. However, they are now a "breed in themselves" and we are beginning to see common issues and trends emerge, many of which are discussed in this book.

Although there are some consistencies between license agreements, most are distinct and unique from one another, and from licensed content to licensed content. Each license must be examined and evaluated on its own. There are similarities in structure, definitions, and terms and conditions addressed in these licenses. As licenses become even more commonplace, it is possible that some standards will emerge, but it is impossible to predict when this might occur and to what degree industry standards may arise for library license agreements.

One reason there is no industry standard in this area is that licensing digital content is relatively new, and with constantly changing technology it is not yet possible to have a single standard. Equally important is the fact that every library, even two similar libraries, may in fact have different needs and therefore may require different license agreements. In addition, each licensed content may require a different arrangement of licensing terms and conditions. This is all due to the needs of researchers and patrons, different available technologies, as well as business and legal reasons (i.e., different lawyers may have different opinions, and different libraries may have different copyright, acquisition, and privacy policies).

MODEL LICENSES AND LICENSING PRINCIPLES

As libraries increasingly license digital content, the question arises whether the process would be simplified by using model licenses or standard agreements that provide uniform licensing conditions. In fact, at the time of writing, there are a handful of model licenses, which are discussed below. In addition, there are licensing principles endorsed by various library associations, also discussed below. Positive and negative aspects of model licenses and licensing principles, as well as tips on how best to use them, are also set out below.

Be careful to understand that model licenses and licensing principles are *not* industry standards. Industry standards are licensing terms and conditions that arise from the consistent use of clauses from library to library, and from content owner to content owner. Model licenses and licensing principles are "ideal" licenses with terms and conditions that library associations and others recommend and which are often worded to the benefit of libraries as opposed to content owners.

Positive Aspects of Model Licenses and Licensing Principles

The benefits of model licenses and licensing principles are as follows:

Industry consistency. Organizations involved in a given industry (i.e., special libraries or public or academic libraries) may use standard agreements similar or equal to those used by their "competitors" in order to increase industrywide efficiency and improve client/patron access to online content. Although no industry standard may exist, consistencies in various terms and conditions in licenses help both sides in negotiating these licenses.

Checklist of issues. By using model licenses and licensing principles as checklists of the possible licensing issues, your library can gain an overall perception of the important issues to consider in your own licenses.

Reduction in "negotiation" time. Time may be saved in situations where similar or equal agreements are negotiated on an ongoing basis between a library and a content owner.

Cost savings. By saving time in negotiations, there are also savings in expenses. Furthermore, by using model licenses or by following licensing principles, there may also be savings in lawyers' fees. However, you should always consult a lawyer if you need an interpretation of a specific legal issue.

Reduction of legal risk. The use of model agreements prepared in advance by a legal professional may reduce potential legal risks that may otherwise be present in situations where contracts are drawn up on an ad hoc basis, by individuals without legal training.

Internal consistency. By using model licenses or by following licensing principles, an organization may ensure that its clients/patrons have equal access to various types of online content. It also becomes easier for the library to manage that license and ensure the use of content according to the terms and conditions of the license.

Potential for flexibility. By using schedules and annexes attached to the agreement, a library may incorporate a significant degree of flexibility into a standard agreement. Clauses that remain the same from agreement to agreement can be placed in the body of the agreement, whereas clauses that may vary in different arrangements with publishers can be reflected in a schedule attached to the agreement.

User-friendly. Model licenses may be drafted in plain English so non-lawyers have a better understanding of their terms and conditions.

Greater certainty. When following a model license or licensing principles, an organization is less concerned about legal issues and can focus instead on accessing the content it requires.

Negative Aspects of Model Licenses and Licensing Principles

There are some negative aspects to model licenses and licensing principles:

Lack of flexibility. If the model licenses or licensing principles are not flexible (i.e., in providing alternative clauses for various situations), problems may arise. Also, a model license may not address all of the specific needs of your organization. There are some circumstances where even the most flexible license will not meet the needs of the situation.

Legal issues. Because of their convenient nature, model licenses are more susceptible to abuse in situations where the other side may claim that its attention was not drawn to a specific term of the contract.

Neglect and undue reliance. Because model licenses and licensing principles are often preprepared and easily printable, users of them may neglect to ensure that the models are updated regularly to reflect changing circumstances, including changes in the law, technology, or licensing practices.

Best Uses of Model Licenses and Licensing Principles

One of the best uses of model licenses or licensing principles is as an educational tool. Examine the clauses in the model license and the principles that best fit your needs. Then examine each term and condition to determine whether it is applicable to your situation. Consider what other clauses you would like in your agreement to fit your particular needs. Read the agreement from start to finish. Ensure that the additions and deletions from the model agreement or licensing principles result in a comprehensive and logical agreement that fits your needs.

A model license and a set of licensing principles also serve as a good checklist of negotiation points. Make sure that your discussions with the content owner include all of the important elements in the model license and in the licensing principles. Remember, the specifics of any particular point that work for your library may be different from the model license or principles.

Model licenses may be very helpful when you are involved in licensing situations with similar terms taking place, and the major variation is the content being licensed. However, always be cautious with any model or standard agreement, as you may find that different content requires variations of terms and conditions. For example, if you license a database, your authorized users may include one group of users, whereas a license for an online journal may include a different group of users. The bottom line is to be aware of your own particular circumstances.

Existing Model Licenses

It may be useful to examine existing model licenses, some examples of which are set out below. As with many licenses, the more recently they have been drafted, the more likely they are to reflect the most up-to-date law, technology, and licensing arrangements.

The Liblicense Standard Licensing Agreement (www.library.yale.edu/~llicense/standlicagree.html) specifically reflects the particular concerns of the university library community and academic publishers. The agreement contains clauses that directly address several issues of particular concern to university librarians: interlibrary loan of digital information, variations in pricing models for digital information, and specific uses of digital information encountered in the university library environment. Although intended for a specific audience, this agreement would be helpful to all who are licensing digital content. The agreement was released in May 2001.

The four model licenses available for free at www.licensingmodels.com were designed for single academic institutions; academic consortia; public libraries; and corporate, government, and other research libraries. The licenses are international in application and were developed in consultations with librarians, publishers, and subscription agents. These licenses were developed by international publishing consultant John Cox and were first made available on the Web in August 1999. A second version, based on further discussions with users of the licenses, was released in May 2000.

In drafting the model licenses, Cox said that "the two most controversial aspects of the licenses undoubtedly concerned the definition of 'authorized users'—remote access, walk-in users, etc.—and the right to use the electronic files to supply copies to other libraries (i.e., interlibrary loan). The licenses give alternatives that reflect the likely outcome of discussion on these issues. It should be noted that it is not the job of the license to indicate a preferred provision, but only to provide the tool in the form of words to be used once agreement has been reached."

The National Electronic Site Licence Initiative has another good model license (www.nesli.ac.uk/nesli8a.html), which is based on a draft model agreement by the Joint Information Systems Committee and Publishers Association (www.ukoln.ac.uk/services/elib/papers/pa/licence/Pajisc21.html).

Existing Licensing Principles

As with model licenses, it may be helpful to examine existing licensing principles, a few examples of which are set out below. As with any document related to licensing digital content, the more recently the principles have been drafted, the more likely they are to reflect the most up-to-date law, technology, and licensing arrangements.

The International Federation of Library Associations and Institutions approved a set of licensing principles in March 2001 that are available at http://www.ifla.org/V/ebpb/copy.htm. These principles deal with such issues as licensing and the law, access and use, end users, perpetual access, pricing, interlibrary loan, and teaching and learning. They are intended for all sorts of libraries, including public, academic, special, and national ones.

In 1997 the Association of Research Libraries published a booklet entitled *Licensing Electronic Resources*, which sets out various principles and issues relevant to licensing by libraries. It is available at http://www.arl.org/scomm/licensing/licbooklet.html.

COLLECTIVE SOCIETIES AND DIGITAL LICENSING

In copyright parlance, a collective society is a group of copyright holders who band together to provide one-stop shopping for users of copyright-protected materials. There are collectives around the world representing rights holders of musical works, print works, artistic works, and other copyright material. Photocopying (or reprography) collectives around the world are either licensing or preparing to license electronic rights to electronic text. Collective societies for other types of works are also beginning to license electronic content. Collective societies can play an important part in digital licensing by simplifying the process for users such as librarians and by providing "one-stop shopping," while at the same time providing rights holders such as content owners with a centralized, and possibly augmented, distribution of their works. With the growth of e-commerce, the question arises as to whether copyright collectives will play a greater role in the digital world, or whether individuals will directly license their own works.

The list that follows describes what several reprography collective societies in North America are doing in the digital world. Many collective societies which have licensed only print or analog works are now beginning to license digital works. In the area of reproducing print works or text, the International Federation of Reproduction Rights Organisations unites reprography collective societies around the world. Its Web site, at http://www.ifrro. org, provides general information on reprography collectives and some general copyright information as well as a useful newsletter. It also has links to reprography collective societies in countries around the world.

United States

COPYRIGHT CLEARANCE CENTER (CCC)

The Copyright Clearance Center, Inc. (www.copyright.com), licenses just about everything, from newspaper and journal articles and the like to course packs or handouts, e-reserve materials, and distance learning copyright material. There are several different packages to choose from the CCC, including academic and business copyright packages. There is some digital content in regard to the e-reserves and such, and because of the Electronic Course Content Service (ECCS) that they offer.

The ECCS includes the Republication Licensing Service (RLS). The RLS (www.copyright.com/ Help/RLSFAQ.htm) licenses rights to republish copyright works in electronic and print media. The CCC obtains rights for different types of electronic media, such as Internet, intranet, CD-ROM, and e-mail.

Canada

CANCOPY

CANCOPY (www.cancopy.com) is the Canadian equivalent of the CCC for English-language print materials in Canada. It recently took over the operations of The Electronic Rights Licensing Agency (TERLA), which was a collective formed to develop digital licenses for the works of Canadian freelance journalists, photographers, and illustrators for use in databases, Web sites, CD-ROMs, and other multimedia formats. CANCOPY is involved with some digital licensing and hopes to expand these activities in the future.

COPIBEC

COPIBEC (www.copibec.qc.ca), the Canadian equivalent of the CCC for French-language print materials, deals with e-rights on a case-by-case basis, in consultation with the rights holders concerned.

NOTE

1. For further information on e-commerce for libraries, see http://copyrightlaws.com regarding the E-LAM Reports on e-commerce for librarians, archives, and museums.

READY TO ROLL

With this brief introduction to the world of digital licensing, I hope that you are ready to proceed to the essentials of licensing and beyond presented in the subsequent chapters of this book.

Demystifying
the Licensing Experience

It's not what I do, but the way I do it.
It's not what I say, but the way I say it.

—Mae West

Licensing involves three simple steps. First, you must determine your library's and its patrons' needs. Second, you must understand the needs of the electronic publisher or content owner. Third, you must find a reasonable compromise between the needs of your library and the content owner.

Keeping it simple is the premise of this book.

THREE STEPS TO NEGOTIATING A LICENSE

STEP ONE
Developing a Licensing Needs Assessment

Your best friend in the licensing process is a blank piece of paper. This may sound odd, but the way I recommend you enter into any new licensing relationship is to start with a blank piece of paper and a pencil—or a blank screen on your computer—and begin writing down all the things you want out of this agreement. Never begin a licensing relationship by reviewing the license itself. The agreement is a document which should summarize all your discussions and negotiations and should never be your starting point. The agreement is often full of legal and technical terminology that can easily distract you from some of the essential and initial points of a license which you need to consider.

NEEDS-BASED LICENSING

You should always know what you want to accomplish before beginning any new license negotiation or drafting.

Figuring out what your needs are, what you need to accomplish, is straightforward and similar to any other RFP (request for proposal) process or other decision-making processes used by librarians. For example, for a new automatic system, you would not start with an RFP, but with a needs assessment. Most collections management assessments start with looking at what you have in your collection and defining what your patrons need—not with the latest reviewing journals or notices from your jobber. (The review journals are full of positive reviews, color pictures, possible discount offers, and "must have" items, and are probably not the best place to start creating a collections list, since this kind of information may distract you from your patrons' information needs.)

To get you started in filling up your blank paper, a list of questions or points you should consider is provided below. They should be seen as a way to guide your discussions with others in your library so that you are directed in your consultations. Consult with your colleagues in responding to these questions and make sure that your points include the different perspectives of various people in your library. Negotiating a license is a group effort within your institution and will have implications for various parts of that institution. Some people to be consulted include librarians (reference and acquisitions librarians are very helpful), library director, legal counsel, the purchasing department, and your information systems office.

It is a good idea to obtain feedback from your patrons as to how the licensed material is to be used. Acquiring a database is no different than acquiring a journal or monograph for a library, since you need to identify not only what information your patrons need, but also in what form they need to make it most accessible and usable.

It is best for one person to coordinate all of this consulting in order to ensure an organized approach to your licenses. It is also best for one person to be the lead negotiator for purposes of consistency.

The points below are the key usage, practical, and strategic points you will inevitably face when signing a license agreement. You may also find it helpful to continually be in the process of creating and amending a licensing policy (see below), which will refine the following questions and add other key questions.

KEY LICENSING ISSUES

Product-Related Issues

Why do you want to license this content?

What are the competitive products to the one you are licensing? Would you be interested in licensing these other products if you cannot agree on suitable terms and conditions for the content you want to license?

What content are you licensing? Include title, ISBN or ISSN, and a brief description of the content.

Do you already subscribe to this same product in print, and are there any financial or negotiation advantages to be gained by this?

In what format will the electronic content be provided to you? On CD-ROM, through the publisher's server, via an intranet, etc.?

How often will you obtain updates to the electronic material? How will these updates be delivered to you?

Does your library require some archival rights after the termination of the license?

User-Related Issues

Who will be using this content? For example, will the users be library staff, patrons, members, faculty, students, alumni, visiting professors, or the public?

How will the content be used? Will it be printed, downloaded, stored electronically, e-mailed to others, etc.?

What uses will be made of this content? Internal, external, Web site, intranet, access through on-premises computers?

What sort of access is necessary? From a single machine, from a library, remote access on campus, in the state, the country, or from other countries?

How many people must be able to access the content at any one time? How many simultaneous users need to access the content?

Library-Related Issues

Will authentication of authorized users be necessary? Is your library able to do this easily and inexpensively? Will the content owner set this up for you?

What mechanisms do you have in place to ensure user confidentiality?

Will you require the need to make a copy for interlibrary loan? By e-mail or by print?

How can your library ensure the content is used according to the terms and conditions of the license? Keep in mind that it will probably be impossible for you to police the use of the content by those accessing it from your library.

What is your library's budget for this content? A range may be more appropriate than an exact dollar amount. You may also want to break up the costs into setup cost, storage cost, maintenance cost, etc.

Will any additional hardware or software be required in order to access the content, and who would be responsible for the related additional costs of these?

What is your preference for payment schemes? Flat rate, pay-per-use, subscription basis, etc.?

Will the electronic publisher provide you with documentation and support for using the content?

Does the electronic publisher warranty how it will address downtime when access to the content will not be possible? Or if some of the content is removed from the database?

License-Related Issues

What duration of the license would work for you?

Would you want the license to automatically renew?

Under what circumstances would you like to be able to terminate the license?

What state/province and country's law should govern the license?

Are there any special circumstances you need to include in the license concerning this content?

Administrative Issues

Who will be negotiating the license? Or will it be a team of negotiators (in which case, who is your primary negotiator)?

Who will be responsible for ensuring the terms and conditions in the license agreement are met during the duration of the license?

How will you keep track of this license and manage your other licenses?

Who will sign the license?

STEP TWO
What Is Being Offered to You?

Once you have filled up your blank page, your next step is to read the license agreement offered to you (assuming one is offered to you). To determine what is being offered to you, you may need to carefully review chapters 3, 4, and 5 of this book, as together these chapters discuss essential licensing concepts and specific terms and conditions set out in licenses. Always ask the content owner about clauses you do not understand—the content owner can be your most valuable source in understanding what is being offered to you.

COMPARE AND CONTRAST

Once you are comfortable in understanding what is being offered to you, you should make notes comparing your initial blank page notes and what is set out in the license. Identify sections of the license that work for you, and ones that require editing. Make a list of items that are missing from the license which you would like to see added to it. These additions may later fit into existing sections of the agreement, or may require new sections to be added to the license.

STEP THREE
Your Negotiated License

Step 3 involves discussing with the content owner how to find a compromise between what works for you and what is being offered to you. Chapter 6 provides helpful tips to guide you through this stage of negotiation. Always keep in mind throughout your discussions that there is no such thing as a "correct" license agreement. The best type of agreement is one with which both the library and content owner are satisfied.

Negotiating a license may be an art and skill in itself. It may be helpful for you to consult resources on negotiation, or even brush up your skills with a course in this area.

DOES YOUR LIBRARY NEED A LICENSING POLICY?

A licensing policy can be a valuable tool for digital collections management. It can make licensing much easier in your institution by providing a more consistent licensing process. A good policy ensures that your library has examined relevant licensing issues before entering into any new licensing arrangements. It also ensures that "one librarian's memory" is not at the root of your library's licensing strategy and acquisition of electronic materials. With a licensing policy, you have a written document that is the basis for all licenses entered into by your library.

Many libraries already have acquisition policies to guide their collection management. Your licensing policy may be part of this policy, or it may be a document on its own.

THREE STEPS TO CREATING A LICENSING POLICY

Your licensing policy should set out the minimum requirements in any license agreements you enter into. When licensing content, you will have to decide based on the circumstances what the appropriate type of arrangement is and how you should set this out in your agreement. At one extreme is a simple document identifying the parties, the works being used, the purpose of their use, length of use, payment, the rights being licensed, a warranty that states the works are in fact owned by the party who is licensing them, and signatures of both parties. At the other extreme may be a twenty-page agreement full of legal terminology. In any licensing situation, you must examine your own perspectives and goals, as well as take into account those of the other party, and tailor your negotiations and agreements to match your particular circumstances.

STEP ONE
Ask Questions

When developing your licensing policy, you may want to start with the minimum requirements of a basic license agreement:

- Who are the parties to the agreement?
- What content is being licensed?
- How will the content be used?
- How long will the content be used?
- How much will the content cost?

- What rights are being licensed (i.e., what uses will be made of the content)?
- What are the warranties from the content provider?

It may be easiest to address these complex issues by responding to the questions set out previously in the "Key Licensing Issues" section of this chapter.

STEP TWO
Review Existing Licenses

Once you have started with the basic requirements of a license agreement, you may then wish to examine various licenses to which you have entered, and mark down all of the consistent points from license to license. Then you may want to mark down all the terms and conditions that vary from license to license. It may be helpful to examine what clauses you liked and did not like in previous agreements. It is also worth noting clauses you found were not workable once the license was signed, or ones that limited your access to the content in any manner. You might include circumstances under which you need to deviate from your minimum requirements, as well as provide a list of circumstances in which you are flexible and may be open to various negotiable clauses.

A helpful part of your licensing policy will set out how new licenses or proposed license arrangements are reviewed and approved within your institution. It should also set out who is involved in which stage or stages of the licensing process.

A licensing policy is not developed overnight. It takes time to create, and may require an amendment after each new license you sign. Amendments to the policy may be required on a regular basis, and may therefore be subject to a regular (e.g., monthly or quarterly) review. If you do not have continual access to a copyright lawyer to help you prepare and update your policy, it may be a good idea to have a lawyer review the policy periodically for both legal issues and for licensing and negotiation strategies. You may also wish to set up a review committee to periodically review and suggest amendments to your licensing policy.

STEP THREE
Review Models

Often model licenses and licensing principles can serve as helpful tools in developing licensing policies and as documents setting out the various issues that you may want to discuss in your licensing negotiations. Model licenses and licensing principles are discussed in chapter 1.

The following example of a draft licensing policy is for a fictional library, the ABC Library. This is a very simple policy and is a good starting point. Yours, however, may be more detailed, especially after it has been revised a number of times to take into account new licenses into which you have entered.

LICENSING POLICY FOR ABC LIBRARY

I. Purpose of Policy

The purpose of this policy is to educate ABC Library staff about licensing basics and to provide a consistent procedure for licensing content for the library. It is not intended to act as a substitute for legal advice, and proper legal advice should be obtained when necessary.

II. What Is a License Agreement?

A license agreement is a written contract between a user and a content owner that sets out the terms and conditions under which a user can use content. As a content owner, you require a license agreement whenever someone else wants to use your content. As a user of content, you need a license agreement whenever you use the content of others. For example, if the library wishes to use a piece of artwork on its Web site, the library must enter into a license agreement with the artist to do so. A license agreement will be necessary for accessing online journals and electronic databases.

III. Basics of License Agreements

As license agreements are legal contracts, it is important to know the basics of contract law. A contract will help to set out the relationship between the parties and can help avoid future conflict. It sets out the rights and obligations of each party.

Contract Basics

A valid contract has the following three components:

An offer to do something or refrain from doing something (e.g., to purchase a book or to license software);

Acceptance of the offer;

Consideration. Consideration is of some value in the eyes of the law. Money is a common form of consideration. However, a promise to perform a service or supply goods is another form.

Common Clauses in License Agreements

It is important to note that license agreements are open to considerable creativity by the parties involved. However, it is important that a license agreement contain the following basic clauses:

Parties to the contract. A license agreement should state the legal names and address of the parties who are subject to the agreement.

Purpose of the contract. The purpose of the license agreement should be set forth. For example, to license software, photographs, or artwork.

Rights and obligations of each party. The rights and obligations of each party should be set out in the license agreement. For example, the artist is to provide the library with a picture on diskette for the library to include on its Web site, while the library must ensure that only library patrons are allowed to view the artwork.

Usage of content. The license agreement should set forth how content can be used and how long it can be used. For example, a photograph may only be used on the library's Web site for a period of one year, or an online journal may be accessed for one year.

Compensation. This clause sets out how much compensation will be provided to the content owner for use of materials.

Copyright ownership. The agreement should discuss ownership of copyright. For example, an author retains ownership in software but licenses it to the library for usage.

Warranties. Warranties in a license agreement set out promises that parties have made. For example, the content owner warrants that he is the owner of the content he is licensing to the library.

The license agreement may have a number of general provisions relating to such things as applicable law, arbitration, etc. The library's lawyer will be of assistance in ensuring that these general provisions protect the interests of the library and comply with any other institutional policies.

IV. How to License Content at ABC Library

If you wish to use content that the library does not own, or if another party wishes to use content that the library owns, a license agreement must be negotiated. If you are provided with a license for the use of digital content that seems to be complete and not subject to negotiation, the first question you must ask the supplier of that content is whether *the license is negotiable*. Even if the content owner says that the license is not negotiable, if there are terms and conditions in the license that do not work for the library, try to amend these clauses. Often, even apparently nonnegotiable licenses are negotiable.

Before negotiating a license agreement, it is important to first determine whether the library has entered into a similar license agreement. This can be done by looking at the ABC Library Licensing Binder, which has categorized all of our agreements by subject area (i.e., Web site, software, journals, periodicals, database, etc.) as well as by name of the publisher/content owner. It is also worth double-checking to ensure the license does not conflict or overlap with existing licenses, including ones to which you are bound through a consortium.

If you find similar content has been licensed in a previous contract, examine the clauses in that other agreement, and find out if any of the clauses were problematic for the parties involved. For example, did the library run into problems with usage restrictions imposed by the content owner that prevented patrons from accessing material? If the similar content was not covered in a previous contract, then look at other agreements in the binder to see if the arrangements between the parties are similar to the type of arrangement you wish to have. Determine how this new situation differs from previous arrangements and if there were any problems in the past that you can avoid this time.

Write down the basics that you wish to have covered by your new license agreement. Ensure that you speak with the library's lawyer (who may or may not have experience in copyright law), the acquisitions librarian, the budget office, and the reference librarian. Before developing any kind of license agreement, it is important to talk to a copyright lawyer (who may or may not be the same person as your library's lawyer). You can discuss what sorts of clauses did not work in past license agreements and get an idea of how to resolve these problems in the future.

It is important to remember that license agreements will differ and will need to be adapted to meet the changing needs of the library. Before signing a license agreement, review its wording carefully to ensure that you know what it means, and consult the library's copyright lawyer to ensure that you are clear on its meaning.

Frequently Asked Questions

[The "frequently asked questions" section of the policy should set out questions that arise from each licensing arrangement. Chapter 7 provides a number of questions and answers that would be useful to add here, but you should continue to update this section with questions that arise in your library.]

Updated [insert date]

GLOBAL ISSUES IN LICENSING CONTENT

Because licensing digital content by its very nature implies global licensing (e.g., content that may be accessed from a Web site from anywhere in the world), there are a number of global copyright and licensing issues of which you should be aware.

Governing Law in Your License

To begin with, you must first determine what laws apply to the license agreement. For example, if your library is in Florida and you are licensing content from a graphic artist or database publisher in British Columbia, should the laws of Florida and the United States or the laws of British Columbia and Canada apply to your agreement in the event of a dispute? When negotiating a license agreement with a content provider in another jurisdiction—whether in another state, province, or country—you will need to determine, discuss, and possibly negotiate which laws apply to the agreement. In the event of a dispute, it will then be clear to both parties which laws apply to resolve the dispute. You probably prefer to have the laws of your own jurisdiction apply to the agreement, as they are likely more familiar to you. This is also discussed in the "Governing Law" section of chapter 5.

International Treaties and Digital Content

Notwithstanding what the agreement states with your content provider, you also want to be aware of copyright issues in countries where the licensed content might be accessed. It is possible that the laws of those countries may apply to the use of the licensed content. For example, disputes arising from your license agreement will most likely be settled according to the laws of the country set out in the license. However, if there are issues of nonauthorized use by third parties, then you have to turn to copyright laws, as opposed to the license, to resolve these issues. This is because the license only governs the parties who sign the license and therefore not necessarily all persons who may have access to the licensed content.

So how does international copyright law work if the license does not govern the use of the content? International copyright protection does not exist in any formal manner. Instead, each country has its own copyright laws. Although international copyright law does not exist per se, there are a number of international treaties that will help you understand how this area of the law works.

The leading international copyright treaty is the Berne Convention. It provides a minimum level of copyright protection. This level of protection is incorporated into the domestic laws of those countries that have joined this convention. This treaty relies on the concept of national treatment. This means that each country that has signed the treaty has to provide authors from other signatory countries the same copyright treatment that it provides to its own citizens. For example, since Canada and Australia are both signatories, Canadian authors will receive the same protection for their works in Australia as Australian authors would. The United States is also a signatory to the convention. A list of member countries of the Berne Convention can be found at http://wipo.int (locate the Berne Convention, then search for contracting parties to the convention).

Two new treaties were developed and drafted in 1996 under the auspices of the World Intellectual Property Organization (WIPO): the WIPO Copyright Treaty and the WIPO Performances and Phonograms Treaty. These treaties are designed to protect the rights of authors whose works are used on the Internet and in other types of new technologies. These treaties will only come into force after ratification by thirty countries each. As of early 2001, neither treaty had been ratified by thirty countries, and the European Union has been urged by the WIPO to ratify these treaties in the near future.

When licensing digital content from international content providers, it is a good idea to determine what treaties are binding not only on your country, but those that are binding on the country of your content provider. This will give a good indication of the level of copyright protection afforded to digital content.

Other Global Issues

Global licensing also involves negotiations and inclusion in your license of the currency used for copyright payments or license fees, applicable taxes, and any considering rights that may not exist in your own country but that exist in other countries (such as moral rights, which exist in European Union countries but only exist minimally in the United States). Another important aspect is your definition of "territory"; i.e., to which countries does the license apply? Equally important are your definitions of such terms as "authorized user," "authorized site," and "on-site use"—these terms will help clarify whether a user may access your intranet from another country on a temporary basis (i.e., while traveling abroad), or through related companies or libraries. These and other related issues are discussed in greater detail in subsequent chapters of this book.

TWELVE MISCONCEPTIONS ABOUT LICENSE AGREEMENTS

Licensing information such as an electronic journal or a database involves entering into a legally binding contract with a rights holder. Although license agreements may appear daunting, they are becoming a fact of life for many who work in libraries. As noted earlier, the processes and concepts behind and involved in setting up a license agreement have a lot in common with the more traditional functions of collections management and library automation. A license agreement merely sets out the terms and conditions for use of specified content and should reflect what the parties have agreed to during their discussions.

The following twelve common misconceptions regarding license agreements will hopefully guide you toward better licenses and less daunting experiences.

1. "A license means permanent ownership."

   This is false. When you license a CD-ROM or a book from a publisher, the publisher is merely allowing you to use the content for a specific purpose. The publisher is not assigning copyright or permanent ownership of the content to you. It is a license to use content, not a transfer of ownership.

2. "Lawyers always negotiate licenses."

   Not long ago, a librarian was responsible for providing access to information. However, with the proliferation of electronic content, librarians are often called upon to negotiate licenses. Licensing has now become a part of the job for many librarians, as well as for those working in archives and museums. In many situations, librarians are more experienced than lawyers in licensing, as they often deal with licensing on a daily and practical basis. Librarians are also often responsible for ensuring compliance with licenses, and again, are forced to understand their complexities.

3. "Renegotiating each year is a necessity."

   It is not necessary to renegotiate your licenses on a yearly basis. Negotiating with a content owner is time-consuming and costly. If both you and the content owner are happy with the license, why should you reopen negotiations? If an automatic renewal clause does not exist in the license, suggest one that would allow the license to automatically renew on the same terms and conditions for a further year, unless either party has given notice, for example, within ninety days of the expiration of the license.

4. "Librarians have no choice but to fight with content owners over licenses."

It is best to work with content owners and rights holders who are fair and reasonable with the terms and conditions they offer you in their licenses. If a content owner is not flexible enough to be open to your needs, then consider licensing from other content owners. If you cannot obtain the access you need for your patrons, then the electronic product loses much of its value to you. For example, if you are licensing a CD-ROM on medicinal plants for your library and the content owner will only allow library staff (and not the public) to use the CD-ROM, you may want to work with another content owner.

5. "Content owners all charge the same way."

All content owners do not charge the same way. Some content owners are willing to charge on a per-use basis. As long as your university or institution can effectively count the number of people accessing or printing the content, you may be able to negotiate payment per-use. In other cases, payment may be based on estimates of the number of users, or based on which print subscriptions you also receive. Some content owners may charge one fee for those with a print and electronic subscription, and a different fee for electronic subscriptions only. How much you pay and the method of payment will depend upon what works for the parties involved. There are no set rules or standards. Choose a method that works the best for your organization and for the content owner.

6. "The term 'user' is always defined by the content owner."

A "user" refers to who can use the content you are licensing. For example, in a university library, you would want students and professors to be able to use content for their courses. Although "user" is often defined by the content owner, the library may need to redefine this term according to its own needs. "User" must be defined in each particular case according to who is actually accessing the content being licensed. Is it the public or members only, or perhaps students and professors? It is important that the definition of "user" be broad enough to encompass all individuals who require access to the content.

7. "The library is responsible for its users."

   Although this may be stated in a license, it is not necessarily the case. The content owner may request that the library be responsible for ensuring that all of its patrons or "users" abide by the license agreements. The content owner may also want you to keep statistics regarding content usage. A librarian is not a police officer! Do not allow the content owner to define the terms of what is suitable enforcement, and do not allow him to hold you liable for patron abuses. At most, agree to a clause that obligates you to notify the content owner should you see any possible violation of copyright in relation to the content. However, you should not have to take positive steps to police the use of licensed content. Always keep in mind that just because the content owner presents you with a license, you do not have to agree with everything in that license, and in certain areas you should be insistent that unreasonable obligations on your part be deleted from the license.

8. "Licenses do not allow for protection of user privacy."

   This is not necessarily true. You may be asked to track usage of the licensed content by your patrons, which could raise a question of privacy. Monitoring how and when your patrons use materials may be considered an invasion of user privacy. If you are concerned with protecting user privacy, you should not agree to track usage by your patrons. If you do agree to track usage of the content, it is a good idea to inform your patrons about this practice and allow them to determine whether or not they choose to use the materials.

9. "Licenses and interlibrary loan are not related."

   Interlibrary loan (ILL) is a component of many license negotiations. One of the main functions of libraries is to share information, and ILL or sharing information with other libraries is a big part of that. You should be ready to negotiate with the content owner as to how you want ILL to operate. Content owners have very different expectations in this area, from no ILL at all to allowing the host institution to print and send copies to other libraries. You have to be careful that you do not overcomplicate your ILL process by having too many different standards among your different content owners and licenses, as this can lead to unexpected costs and management issues.

10. "Electronic journals are cheaper than paper ones."

   Electronic journals are not necessarily cheaper than traditional paper journals. Not only will new staff be required to manage the collection (such as negotiating licenses, monitoring licenses, managing computers, etc.), but the library is also paying for the technology needed to access this information. This may involve purchasing new computers, software, or a new server. In addition, patrons may also be paying part of the costs when they access the information and then print it.

11. "You have no control over the format of delivery or storage."

   You do have control over what format the content is being delivered to you and how it is stored. It is important that the content is provided to you in a format that is acceptable to your institution and fits with your technology. Determine what format the information will be provided to you, when it will be provided to you, and if there will be any technical support provided to you if there are problems accessing the information. For example, if you are licensing an electronic journal from a publisher, will the journal be provided to you in CD-ROM format or will you need to access the information from the publisher's server? What if there are defects in the CD-ROM? Keep in mind how you would like these problems to be addressed and set it out in your license.

12. "Fair use or fair dealing do not apply to the electronic environment."

   The concept of fair use or fair dealing by users applies to content in the electronic environment. The content owner may want to limit the fair use or fair dealing by your patrons in the license agreement. However, it is important to note that your patrons are not a party to the license agreement. As a result, they are not bound by the license agreement that you make with the content owner. Although you and the content owner may agree to limit the fair use or fair dealing portions of the applicable copyright act in your license agreement, the library's patrons are still protected by fair use or fair dealing under the act. If the content owner is aware of this, he may want your library to be held responsible for your patrons' actions. Therefore, it is important to ensure that the license does not restrict the fair use/fair dealing of content by your patrons.

ARE YOU DEMYSTIFIED?

Learning about digital licensing is a lengthy process. You may read about licensing, take a course on this topic, discuss it with colleagues, and even negotiate and interpret a few licenses and still feel that you have much to learn. You may take some comfort in the fact that we all have much to learn about licensing. We will have to learn this together as we work with content owners over the next several years in finding licenses that meet all of our needs.

Learning the Lingo

It is important to understand a number of essential concepts found in license agreements before proceeding to a clause-by-clause examination of a license. These concepts are discussed in this chapter and are referred to throughout this book. Many of these concepts are defined in this chapter in a licensing context and may have different meanings in another context.

LICENSES VS. ASSIGNMENTS

Before examining specific terms and conditions in a license agreement, you should have a full understanding of the term "licensing." In simple terms, *licenses* and *assignments* are two ways to use content.

In an assignment situation, a content owner *assigns* his rights. This means that the content owner is permanently giving away his content, or a portion of his content. An assignment is like a sale or a transfer of rights, whereas a license is comparable to a lease or a rental of rights. In a licensing situation, the content owner *licenses* a piece of his or her content, thereby temporarily permitting someone else to use it.

Using the words "assignment" or "license" may not by themselves guarantee what types of rights are being granted. The wording used in a license agreement could be such that, in practice, it has a similar effect to an assignment. The key concept to understand is that rights may be exploited (usually in exchange for money) without necessarily being sold or permanently given away to someone else. For example, your library could license the rights to a database even though your library has no permanent or ownership rights in that database.

When you are involved with license agreements, you may hear the term "purchaser" of content being referred to in both assignment and licensing situations, even though there is no actual change of ownership in a license situation. This is because the "purchaser" purchases the right to use content in a certain manner even though he or she may not acquire outright ownership of that right or content. Similarly, the term "buying and selling" content may refer to licensing content. These are terms and meanings used in the marketplace and something of which you should be aware.

LICENSE AGREEMENT

A license agreement is a legally binding contract between two parties. The license is a legal term for *permission* to use or access copyright-protected material. In this book, a "license agreement" or "contract" means a written document setting out mutually acceptable terms and conditions under which a library may use electronic or digital content owned by someone else. If you are licensing digital content like books, periodicals, and databases, the license agreement will set out the conditions of use of the digital content—at a specific price for a specified period of time.

UNDERSTANDING THE LINGO

Digital Licensing

"Digital licensing" means the licensing arrangement containing the particular circumstances under which a content owner and user, such as a library, agree upon the use of, or access to, specified electronic content. The details agreed upon are usually set out in a written form called a "license agreement" or "contract." In simpler terms, a "license agreement" or "contract" are terms used for *permission* to use certain content.

Content

For the purposes of this book, "content" refers to the works being licensed, such as electronic books, periodicals, journals, databases, news feeds, encyclopedias, images, Web site content, and the like.

Licensor

A *licensor* is the owner of the electronic content. A licensor may be a photographer or periodical writer. A licensor may also be the publisher of a database or periodical or journal. A library may also be a licensor, for example, if the library owns the copyright to manuscripts. Generally, the licensor owns the content and can legally allow others to use that content.

Licensee

A *licensee* is the person or entity who obtains permission to use the electronic content. For example, a licensee may be a library, educational institution, or resource center which licenses content from the licensor.

Content Owner

The *content owner* is the person or entity that created the content being licensed, or that has acquired the ownership of the content from the actual creator of it. For the purposes of this book, a content owner can also be a person or entity who has permission from the original creator of the work to license the work to libraries and others, such as a publisher, aggregator, or vendor (who makes a number of databases available for use). When licensing content from a publisher, aggregator, or vendor who does not actually own the rights to the content, you want a guarantee that they actually have the right to license you the content. This should be carefully set out in the warranty and indemnity sections of your license, as discussed in chapter 4. A content owner is sometimes referred to as a "content provider."

Exclusivity

The rights granted in a license may be *nonexclusive* or *exclusive*. "Nonexclusive" means that the owner may grant another organization the right to use the same material. For example, Publisher X may grant the right to use its content to Library A, Library B, and Library C. "Exclusive" means that the publisher may only grant the content to one party/library at any given time. Most digital licenses entered into by libraries are on a nonexclusive basis.

Rights

Rights are the uses permitted under the license. They may include, for example, the right to print a copy of an electronic article, or to access a database.

Fair Use, Fair Dealing, Library Exceptions, and Licensing

This book presumes that the concept of fair use/fair dealing or of various exceptions from copyright law are not applicable to the use of the electronic content you want to license, and therefore you need permission to use the content. However, you may still need to deal with fair use/fair dealing as it applies to patrons accessing the licensed content, as discussed in chapter 4.

Fair use is a concept from the U.S. Copyright Act that acts as a defense should you use copyright-protected works and must defend your use in a court of law. Under Section 107 of this act, the "fair use" of copyright-protected works is not an infringement of copyright. "Fair use" is intended to apply to the reproduction of copyrighted works for such purposes as criticism, comment, news reporting, teaching (including multiple copies for classroom use), and scholarship or research. However, in order to be fair, you must apply the four factors set out in the Copyright Act. You must consider (1) the purpose and character of the use (including whether it is for a commercial or a nonprofit educational purpose); (2) the nature of the copyrighted work; (3) the amount and substantiality of the portion used in relation to the work as a whole; and (4) the effect of the use upon the potential market for or value of the copyrighted work. A copy of Section 107 is provided in appendix A of this book.

Unfortunately, clear rules do not exist for interpreting what use would constitute a fair use. Thus, the concept has been a cause of frustration for many librarians and patrons who attempt to apply it to their situation. Ultimately, it would be up to a court of law to determine whether a use is considered fair.

The concept of fair dealing exists in the law of various countries such as Canada and the United Kingdom. It is a defense for the limited reproduction of copyright works, though it is narrower than the concept of fair use in the United States. It is similar to the fair use concept, however, in that it does not provide clear guidance on what uses of copyright materials may fall under it.

Exceptions from copyright law mean that you do not have to pay to use a copyright work and do not have to obtain permission to use it. Exceptions from copyright law specifically for libraries exist in the United States, Canada, and in the laws of other countries around the world. Generally, these exceptions are for specific uses of copyright materials. It is unlikely that an exception in a copyright statute would ever allow for the free use of an electronic database or electronic journal. Therefore, you would still need a license to use electronic materials in your library.

Privity of Contract

"Privity of contract" is legal terminology for a license only being valid between the parties who sign the agreement. For example, a license is only valid between the library and publisher who sign the license, and a library patron is not subject to the license. Therefore, if a library patron violates any terms and conditions in the license, the publisher has no right to sue the patron for violation of the license. However, there may be rights under the applicable copyright statute for certain uses of licensed content. For instance, if the content is used in a manner that infringes the rights of the copyright holder, and the patron does not have permission to use the content in this way, then the publisher may sue for infringement of copyright, as opposed to violation of the license itself. This is addressed in several sections of chapter 4 such as "Fair Use/Fair Dealing" and "Monitoring Use."

Consortia

For the purposes of this book, a *consortium* is a group of libraries that join together to license one or several electronic resources. Note that there are also consortia of content owners. There are now hundreds and possibly thousands of consortia worldwide. Some consortia charge a fee for membership and other services, while others are free (though they will charge for the actual cost of licensing the electronic resources). Some consortia are for specific types of libraries, while others are for a variety of libraries and may include government, public, academic, school, and special libraries. Libraries often belong to more than one consortium in order to license different electronic products.

Consortia may, but do not necessarily, save libraries money on licensing fees, but they can make the same amount of money go much further. They can also benefit libraries by saving time and legal costs in negotiating licenses and in sharing negotiating expertise.

Each consortium is unique in terms of the content it is licensing, its structure, background, and goals. Joining a consortium is a collections management decision, and you want to ensure that you find the right one to meet your needs and goals. If you join a consortium, make sure it is licensing the content you need, has similar goals to your own library, has a decision-making process that meets your needs, and has a strong lead negotiator.

Further Lingo

The definitions of other words frequently used in licenses or in the negotiation process are provided in a glossary at the end of this book. This list has been compiled by the Yale University Library.

CONTRACTUAL AGREEMENTS

In order to enter into a digital license agreement, you need to know the basic principles of *contract law*. From a lawyer's point of view, a contract or agreement is a tool that clarifies a relationship between the parties, and a document to help those parties avoid future conflict and possible litigation by setting out the terms and conditions of their arrangements in advance. It is a listing of each party's responsibilities or promises with respect to the rights and obligations of each party. It is a document that each party may return to from time to time to verify its original agreement, its rights and obligations, and the rights and obligations of the other party in the particular circumstances. A contract is also a useful tool for identifying all the costs of a project and who is responsible for paying them. Contracts are enforceable in court, or alternatively through mediation or arbitration (as further discussed in chapter 5, "Boilerplate Clauses"), if one party does not live up to its obligations in the agreement.

What Is a Contract?

For the purposes of this book, the terms "contract," "license," and "agreement" are used interchangeably. In legal terms, there is a contract when two or more persons or organizations, often referred to as "parties," agree to exchange something, whether it be a physical or intellectual property or a promise of future performance.

Must the Contract Be in Writing?

Contracts may be oral or in writing, and they may be a distinct document or part of an invoice or purchase order. Oral agreements can be a problem because they rely on the memory and understanding of the parties involved. For example, if librarian Judy orally negotiates a license agreement for a database, then leaves her job, how will her library ensure that it is using the database according to the terms and conditions of the license Judy negotiated on the library's behalf?

In addition to their use as permanent records, written agreements make the parties think carefully about the terms and conditions in the license and be specific about them. Oral contracts are hard to prove, since they are usually one person's word against another's. If you ever have to go to court or arbitration, a written agreement may result in less dispute about the clauses in the license. Written agreements are always advisable.

Although oral contracts may be legally binding in certain circumstances and in certain jurisdictions, this is not universally true. Some contracts must be in writing to be enforced. For example, the U.S. and Canadian copyright statutes require an assignment of copyright or exclusive license to be in writing. Although contract requirements vary from state to state and province to province, many U.S. states require that any contract for the sale of goods for $500 or more be in writing.

What Is a Valid Contract?

When negotiating, drafting, or reviewing a contract, keep in mind that a valid contract has the following three components:

1. an offer to do something or refrain from doing something (e.g., to purchase a print book, license an online database or computer software, or commission someone to design a Web site);
2. acceptance of the offer; and
3. consideration. Consideration is something that is of some value in the eyes of the law. Money is one form of consideration; a promise to supply goods or to perform services is another.

Common Clauses

Any terms and conditions to which the parties agree may be included in the contract, provided they do not contravene any specific laws.

A contract should state the legal names and addresses of the parties who are subject to it. The contract should state the purpose of the contract (e.g., to license an online periodical or database) and the rights and obligations of each party. For example, the publisher will publish an online periodical that the library will license for a two-year period.

Key clauses to include in a license agreement are set out in detail in chapter 4 of this book. The contract may also have a number of general or boilerplate provisions relating to such things as arbitration, applicable law, bankruptcy, etc., which are discussed in chapter 5.

The agreement should be signed by all parties to it. If contracting with a corporation, the signature should be that of an authorized corporate officer. That officer's name, title, and the name of the corporation should be stated. It is also advisable to place the corporate seal on the agreement.

Before signing a contract, review the wording of your contract with great care to ensure that it means only what you think and intend it to mean. Ask the other party for any clarifications, and consider consulting a copyright lawyer before signing on the dotted line.

OTHER RELEVANT LEGISLATION

UCITA

"UCITA" is an acronym for the Uniform Computer Information Transactions Act in the United States. UCITA is a law that has to date only been adopted in two states, Maryland and Virginia. Its purpose is to regulate transactions in intangible goods such as computer software, online databases, and other information products in digital form. Publishers and large software producers are the primary supporters of UCITA. Libraries, consumer protection groups, and certain businesses continue to oppose the enactment of UCITA. One of the complaints of libraries is that UCITA is intended to regulate business-to-business contractual arrangements and that its general application may not specifically address the needs of libraries. Under UCITA, for example, a library, small business, and individual consumer all using the same computer software may be subject to the same license restrictions, although the use of the software may vary greatly for each of these users. For further information on the conflicting concerns of UCITA and libraries, see http://www.ala.org/washoff/ucita/.

Digital Millennium Copyright Act

The Digital Millennium Copyright Act (DMCA) in the United States became largely effective on October 28, 1998. Title I of the DMCA creates significant new remedies against unauthorized circumvention of the technological protection measures that are used to control access and protect exclusive rights in copyright-protected works. It also prohibits deliberate tampering with copyright management information. Title II clarifies the potential liability of Internet service providers (ISPs) for certain copyright infringements by their customers and others. Title IV permits libraries and archives to make digital copies of works for preservation purposes, and amends the ephemeral copy arrangements for the transmission of sound recordings under the U.S. Digital Performance Right in Sound Recordings Act of 1995. For further information, see http://www.ala.org.

YOUR OWN LINGO

As you journey into the world of digital licensing, you will come across many more terms than those discussed in this chapter. In fact, you will soon find that you have learned many new concepts, and perhaps developed a lingo of your own which relates to licensing digital content.

Key Digital
Licensing Clauses

Together, generalized judges and specialized lawyers
can produce intellectual property law that will mellow,
adapt and improve in quality over time, in the spirit
of the fine product produced here in Napa Valley.

—Speech to Copyright Society, February 2000,
Napa Valley (Calif.), by Mary M. Schroeder,
Judge, U.S. Court of Appeals (Ninth Circuit)

Different license agreements are written in different manners: some are as brief as one page, while others are ten pages or longer; and some are written in nontechnical language, while others are filled with legal terminology. This chapter discusses key digital licensing clauses that are common to many licenses. Although each license is unique, the clauses discussed in this chapter may serve as a valuable checklist when examining licenses you are negotiating or interpreting.

Be cautious when comparing the list of clauses in this chapter with your license. Licenses may vary greatly in how they set out the terms and conditions of the licensed content. For example, one license may have a clause dealing solely with rights, while another license may include the rights granted under a more comprehensive clause covering the licensee's obligations or restrictions on use. Before interpreting any one clause, read the entire license you are considering and see how the various terms and conditions are organized and set out. Do not be concerned if your license uses different terminology and headings than those in this chapter. Clauses may have to be added, omitted, and amended to meet your particular circumstances. In many situations, your license may be brief and the details about the clauses may appear in an appendix attached to the license. This is common for definitions, terms, and duration and payment. Also, the order of clauses in a license may vary from agreement to agreement.

GOVERNMENT AGENCIES

When a library is part of a government agency, it may be required to include or exclude specific provisions in its licenses. If your library is part of a U.S. government agency, check with your institution for the specific requirements regarding license agreements.

KEY DIGITAL LICENSING CLAUSES

The clauses discussed in this chapter are set out in an order that is intended to be logical in terms of reviewing an agreement from beginning to end. You may find a different order in your licenses.

- Preamble
- Parties to the Agreement
- Definitions
- Content Covered by the Agreement
- Rights Granted/License
- Sublicenses
- Interlibrary Loan
- Fair Use/Fair Dealing
- E-Rights
- Usage or Authorized Uses
- Usage Restrictions
- License Fee/Payment
- Licensor Obligations
- Delivery and Continuing Access to the Licensed Content
- Support and Documentation

- Library/Licensee Obligations
- Monitoring Use
- Moral Rights
- Credits
- Territory
- Authorized Users
- Authorized Site
- Copyright Ownership
- Duration of Grant of Rights (Term of Agreement)
- Renewal
- Termination
- Perpetual Access/Archive
- Disclaimers
- Warranties
- Indemnity and Limitation of Liability

PREAMBLE

Licensing Tip: A preamble is not mandatory and does not form
part of the license. If there is a preamble in your license, it should
be as concise as possible.

The preamble is the introduction to your license. The preamble sets out the
purpose of the agreement, i.e., for one party to license the content of the
other party. Typically, a preamble sets out identifying information about the
two parties that will sign the agreement, the names of the parties, their
addresses, the name or a brief description of the content being licensed, who
owns the content, and who wants to license the content. It often sets out the
date the agreement becomes effective; alternatively, this may be set out at
the end of the agreement above the signature lines.

A preamble is not considered part of the agreement. However, it may be
referred to should the license later result in any ambiguity and require interpretation.

A preamble may also be called "Background," "Recitals," or "Parties" or
have no title at all. Many licenses, especially shorter ones, do not have a
preamble, nor is one mandatory. Many preambles begin with various
"whereas" statements such as "Whereas the Publisher is the owner of the
rights granted under this License And Whereas the Library wishes to license
these rights, It is agreed as follows . . ." As discussed elsewhere in this book,
it is not necessary to use such legal terminology as long as the clauses in the
license are clearly written and understandable.

PARTIES TO THE AGREEMENT

Licensing Tip: Ensure that the parties are properly identified (by
legal name, address, telephone number, and e-mail address) either
in the preamble or in one of the initial clauses in the license.

A license must clearly set out the names of the two parties entering into the
license. When this is not done in the preamble, it is important that the
license, preferably at the beginning of the agreement, set out identifying
information of the parties. It may also be placed in the notices clause as discussed in chapter 5.

Identifying information includes the following:

the legal names of the parties

snail mail addresses (i.e., postal mailing addresses)

e-mail addresses, telephone and fax numbers (as a convenience in order
to locate the other party during or after the license has been signed.
Although this is not routinely done, it is highly advisable to have all
of this information in the license itself, since much of your correspondence during and after negotiations may be via e-mail.)

The parties to the agreement are the licensor and licensee. The owner
of the digital content is the licensor, e.g., the publisher, content aggregator,
or owner of the content being licensed. The licensee is your library, the party
obtaining access to the digital information (usually for use by end-users—
your library's patrons). Although many licenses will use the terms "Licensor"
and "Licensee" throughout the agreement, it is not necessary to use these
words once the parties have been identified. You may then simply use "the
Library" and "the Publisher" or "the Content Owner," etc., or the names or
abbreviations of the names of the two parties, such as "the Annapolis
Library" and "the River Publishing Co." However, reference to the legal
names of the contracting parties should be included somewhere in the
license. Some libraries are legal entities in themselves and may sign legal
agreements, whereas other libraries are part of larger legal entities.

It is important that both parties have the authority to enter into the
agreement. Before entering into the agreement, be sure to ask the following
questions: does the owner of the digital information have authority to license
the digital information, or does he need to clear rights with another party?
(This is further discussed in the "Warranties" and "Indemnity and
Limitation of Liability" sections of this chapter.) Do you have signing
authority on behalf of your library, and if not, who should be signing the
agreement? Make sure that the name on the license is the one that has legal
authority to enter into legal arrangements. (See also the "Signature" section
in chapter 5.)

DEFINITIONS

Licensing Tip: For each important term used in the license, ask
whether it is being used in the context of its dictionary meaning or
whether it requires a special definition for purposes of the license.

There are no specific standards or universal models for a licensing agreement. Basically, a good licensing agreement is one that is clear to the parties who sign it, and to others who will be interpreting it and applying its terms and conditions to particular circumstances. The agreement should therefore define terms whose meaning may be unclear or which may have more than one meaning.

Terms that you should consider defining include "authorized uses," "authorized users," "commercial use," "content," "interlibrary loan," "licensed content," "premises," and "territory." Note that "authorized uses" and "authorized users" are often not defined in the definition section if they are defined in a separate clause. The basic rule of thumb is that if a word is being used other than in its ordinary dictionary meaning, then include that "special" meaning in the agreement. That meaning should be one agreed upon by both parties to the agreement, and may be part of your license negotiations.

Although the definition section may seem straightforward when reviewing a license offered to you, take the time to carefully review the way terms have been defined. The way words are defined should meet your needs and expectations. The definition may affect other parts of the agreement, and you always want to ensure that you are licensing content in the manner that works for you.

If you have more than one license with the same publisher for different content, you may use different definitions in each license, since the definitions may vary vis-à-vis different content.

The definitions may be set out in a separate section, usually at the beginning of the license, or defined throughout the license. They may also be included in an appendix. Placing all of the definitions in a single location in the license can make it easier to consult that section when coming across various terms in the agreement that are defined in it.

CONTENT COVERED BY THE AGREEMENT

Licensing Tip: Be as specific as possible about the content being licensed. If feasible, attach a copy of the licensed content, or a list of it, to the license.

The clause dealing with content covered by the agreement is often called "Subject," "Subject Matter," or "Product Definition."

It is vital that your agreement is clear as to what content is being licensed. For instance, is your library licensing the electronic version of a print publication to which you subscribe, or an electronic-only periodical? Is the content an online subscription to a journal, database encyclopedia, financial information, or news feed? You may need to define whether such content includes full-text articles, abstracts, a table of contents, indices, and any new or special online products, sections, or services that may only be made available online.

Keep in mind that with digital content there may be more than one type of content which must be covered by the license. Less obvious works and underlying works that may be subject to the license can include text, images, databases, musical and other audio works, video and film clips, computer software, and the like.

If the description of the content is lengthy, some licenses include the description in an appendix attached to the license. For instance, you could include a five-page list of articles which are subject to the license. Also, if the content is brief, for example, a single article or a single image, you may attach a copy of the image or article to the license so it is easily identifiable.

See also the discussion below in the section "Delivery and Continuing Access to the Licensed Content" about a reimbursement of the license fee should content specified in the license no longer be accessible during the duration of the license.

Some licenses state that copyright in the content remains with the content owner. This may also be dealt with in a separate copyright clause as discussed below.

RIGHTS GRANTED/LICENSE

> **Licensing Tip:** Whether your grant of license clause is brief or lengthy, specific or broad, ensure that it allows the necessary access to use the content in the intended manner for your library.

The grant clause or license sets out the rights being granted to the library by the owner of the digital information. It states how the library may use the content being licensed and what uses of the content are prohibited. This clause is sometimes titled "Permission," "Permitted Uses," "Grant of License," or "Authorized Uses."

The rights granted may be *nonexclusive* or *exclusive*. "Nonexclusive" means the owner may grant another individual or organization the right to use the same content. For example, Publisher X may grant the right to use its content to Library A, Library B, and Library C. "Exclusive" means that the publisher may only grant the content to one party/library at any given time. Most digital library licenses are granted on a nonexclusive basis.

Many grants of rights state the license is "nontransferable." This means that the library licensing the content may not transfer its license to another library. This is further discussed in chapter 5 under the "Transferability or Assignment" section.

The grant clause sets out the scope of rights. Rights may be set out narrowly or broadly, depending on what the parties agree upon. An example of a broad license would be a license to use the content in any manner whatsoever for the entire duration of copyright of the content. A narrow license might be the inclusion of a specific chapter of a book on your library's Web site for a sixty-day period.

Generally, library licenses for periodicals, databases, text content, etc., are for specific rights. Libraries are not generally granted, nor do they usually require, the type of broad license exemplified in the preceding paragraph. Since it is unusual in a library setting for all rights to be licensed to you, your license will spell out the specific rights being licensed. There are no special rules or words for setting out these rights—what you want is a clear statement of what the parties have agreed to. Some licenses use terms like "reproduce," "adapt," "transmit," "broadcast," or "perform in public," and other terms are found in various copyright statutes around the world. Still other licenses may use wording relating to the relevant activities, such as "searching," "retrieving," and "printing."

The grant of rights sets out the permitted uses. What uses does your library need to make of the online content you are licensing? Do you need to be able to view, reproduce, store, or save copies during the duration of the paid online subscription (i.e., on a hard drive or other digital information storage medium)? What about the ability to search, browse, retrieve, display, download, print, forward electronically to others, e-mail to oneself, fax to oneself or to a colleague, and include in a Web site, intranet, extranet, local area network (LAN), wide area network (WAN), or other closed network (or in a Web site that is password protected)? These are all things that may be addressed in your agreement.

Without the proper grant of rights, your library may not be able to use the licensed content in the ways needed, and therefore the content is less valuable to you and your patrons. Make sure the license meets your needs and allows you to do all that your library or its patrons require. Otherwise, you may have to make additional payments and obtain additional permissions after signing the license.

The following is a list of rights you may see or want to consider for inclusion in your licenses. Some of the terms set out below may need to be defined in the license agreement. In reviewing various license agreements, rights granted or "permitted uses" often include the rights to:

- View
- Reproduce (sometimes for specific purposes)
- Store or save copies or a certain portion of the licensed content (i.e., on hard drive, floppy disk, backup tape, or any other digital information storage medium)

   This may be temporary storage, in which case your agreement should state the length of permissible storage. In addition, this may include caching, in which a digital copy is made so that the content can be more efficiently distributed to users.

   More rarely, this may include permanent storage. See also the "Perpetual Access/Archive" section in this chapter.

- Search
- Browse
- Retrieve
- Display
- Download (see "Store or save copies," above)
- Print (generally, individual articles or small portions of an electronic product. If the library is printing the article or portion on its premises, the library may negotiate that the license allow the library to charge a fee to cover costs of the printing.)
- Forward electronically to others

Examine your agreement and see what uses are specifically permitted. Are some uses missing? Do you need to include some of these omitted uses or rights? What is your normal use of the content? How about future uses of this content: does the license provide for this, or will you have to return to the content owner for further permission? With the rights granted to you, are you able to carry on with your regular role of providing content to your patrons?

Some agreements list the above rights as being granted specifically in relation to an individual article or portion in an electronic journal or database. Again, ask yourself if this meets the needs of the patrons of your library, or do you and they require broader access?

In addition to the rights granted set out above, there are other permitted uses that you may want included in the grant of rights, such as:

- E-mail to oneself
- Fax to oneself or to a colleague
- Electronic links (to allow the library to link to the licensed content for purposes of its patrons accessing that content)[1]
- Caching (so your library can make a digital copy for purposes of efficiently providing the content to its users)
- Include in an intranet, extranet, LAN, WAN, or other closed network (or Web site that is password protected)
- Include in a Web site (which has public access but is non-commercial in that it is for informational purposes only)
- Interlibrary loan
- Index the contents
- Course packets, training materials (this may include print copies or electronic copies)
- Electronic reserve (this may be for a specific course and will usually only be for a portion of the licensed content)
- Distance learning
- Special uses (e.g., patent or drug applications)
- Load the content onto the library's server[2]
- Make backup copies for a specific period of time[3]

If the licensed content is a database or other compilation or collection of information, your license may specifically state that the rights include extraction and manipulation of information from that database.

Some licenses set out the grant of rights followed by a phrase such as "and all similar uses" or "and related uses," etc. This is advantageous to a library, since the license may thereby include some uses that are not specifically mentioned in its various clauses. However, from the publisher's perspective, it is in its best interests to explicitly state what uses are included in the license agreement, and to explicitly state what uses are *not* included (or to state something to the effect that "all uses not specifically mentioned herein are retained by the publisher"). Licenses more commonly take this latter approach. Although this is less flexible for libraries, it does help to avoid ambiguity in the license.

Who is entitled to these rights is further discussed in the sections entitled "Sublicenses," "Authorized Users," "Authorized Site," "Usage or Authorized Uses," and "Usage Restrictions" in this chapter.

SUBLICENSES

> **Licensing Tip:** Determine all uses of the licensed content that may be made and by whom and include these people as sublicensees.

Generally, a license involves two types of arrangements. The first type is a license, for example, from a database or periodical publisher to your library. The second type, which is also called a "sublicense," would be the license that allows the library to provide the database or periodical to its patrons and possibly even to the public. In other words, a sublicense is a license a library gives to a third party.

Most libraries are licensing content from publishers and other content owners for the purpose of sublicensing it to their patrons and researchers. For example, *Library* magazine may be licensed to Library X, then Library X "sublicenses" the magazine to a library patron or researcher by allowing that patron or researcher to view the contents of the magazine and print an article from it. As such, you should ask yourself and others in your library what sort of access your library patrons and researchers should be entitled to. You may consider all of the applicable rights set out in the rights granted clause, as discussed above. Sublicensees are usually considered "authorized users," and your license may not include clauses for both of these terms. The bottom line is to ensure that whatever terminology is used, any necessary sublicensees are provided for in the license, either in the rights granted clause or in the authorized users clause, or in both clauses.

INTERLIBRARY LOAN

> **Licensing Tip:** If desired, negotiate how an interlibrary loan may fit within your license.

What is an interlibrary loan (ILL)? In simple terms, it is the lending of library materials from one library to another library. Note that an ILL is generally for print materials such as a book, periodical article (though not usually for an entire issue of a magazine), pamphlet, government document, etc. Generally, audiovisual materials like videos, and digital materials like CD-ROMs, computer software, music CDs, and databases are not part of an ILL.

Is electronic interlibrary loan permitted for the content licensed under your agreement? This is something you may have to negotiate if you would like ILL included. At the time of writing this book, the inclusion of ILL is somewhat controversial, and agreements vary on whether to include it or not. One reason it is controversial is because traditional ILL meant that the print documents were shared with another library, then returned to the original library. This procedure may not be applicable to electronic documents, though a vendor allowing ILL may ask that the electronic document be destroyed after having been loaned for a certain period of time to the "borrowing" library. Some licenses that do include an ILL provision make any ILL subject to compliance with the ILL provision in Section 108 of the U.S. Copyright Act. (A copy of Section 108 is provided in appendix B of this book.) The bottom line is that if ILL is something your library requires, then ask for it in your agreement. It may be necessary to define ILL for the purposes of your license, i.e., in an electronic context.

Some publishers will not agree to an electronic ILL provision because they believe that any electronic copy may be distributed around the world in seconds. Although this is a valid fear, it is also very easy to scan a print article and distribute it around the world in seconds. You may want to point this out to a publisher who will allow you to print an article from an electronic database for sharing with another library as an ILL, but will not allow an electronic ILL. Also, publishers' fears on this account may decrease as new computer software and technology ensure greater protection of digital content.

The inclusion of an electronic ILL provision may exist in a variety of forms. For example, your license may allow printing an article from an electronic database, which may then be faxed to another library for ILL purposes. If you subscribe to both the print and electronic version of a journal, the print version may be subject to ILL although the electronic one is not. Or, your license may allow electronic ILL subject to specific and sometimes extensive record-keeping which goes beyond what is normally required for print ILL. Try to negotiate an ILL provision that works best for your library.

FAIR USE/FAIR DEALING

Licensing Tip: If desired, negotiate a fair use/fair dealing provision that meets your needs.[4]

In the United States, license agreements may limit rights that otherwise would apply under the application of the U.S. copyright law and principles of fair use.[5] If an agreement does not discuss fair use or expressly acknowledge it, then the concept of fair use will apply. The same is true in Canada and the United Kingdom and in other countries with a fair dealing provision. However, the agreement may restrict fair use or fair dealing. Note that even if fair use/fair dealing is restricted, it will only be restricted in terms of the library, and not vis-à-vis patrons, as the agreement is only valid between the parties who sign it. This is a controversial issue, and it is something libraries may have difficulty in seeing eye-to-eye with content owners. Explicitly stating that fair use/fair dealing applies may make publishers and content owners appear in a more positive light by libraries. Some licenses that specifically refer to fair use allow it in a manner that is consistent with the fair use provision in Section 107 of the U.S. Copyright Act. (A copy of Section 107 is provided in appendix A of this book.) The same is true in countries which include a fair dealing clause in their copyright statutes.

E-RIGHTS

> **Licensing Tip:** Understand what is encompassed by the broad term "e-rights" and ensure that specific and necessary e-rights are defined and set out in your license.

"E-rights" or "electronic rights" is a term that has become very popular in licensing parlance. E-rights are not, however, specifically defined in the copyright laws of most countries. E-rights would be included as part of more general or flexible rights, such as the right of reproduction, which are set out in copyright laws around the world.

E-rights may include a large variety of rights for such things as using the electronic content found in electronic books, journals, databases, CD-ROMs, DVDs, online, Internet, intranets, extranets, Web sites, and archives. As technology changes, so may the meaning of e-rights, and even the notion of such popular platforms as CD-ROMs and DVDs. If you use the term "e-rights" in your license, it should be defined. For instance, will it include all electronic rights, or just Web rights, or other specific rights? Unless your license does cover all electronic uses, which is unusual, then it should refer to the specific electronic uses that you require and which are set out above in the section "Rights Granted/License."

USAGE OR AUTHORIZED USES

> **Licensing Tip:** Determine in what manner the content will be used and ensure that this is carefully addressed and defined in your license.

License agreements generally specify the purpose of the use of the content for licensing and sublicensing. This is sometimes referred to in licenses as "Authorized Uses," "Conditions of Use," or "Purpose." Usage may include the following:

- Personal
- Noncommercial
- Scholarly
- Research
- Scientific
- Educational
- Review or comment
- Private use or research
- Electronic reserves
- Class packages, training courses
- Internal research in the course of employment, business, or profession

Certain of the concepts set out above may need to be defined for the purposes of your license. For example, terms like "noncommercial use" or "commercial gain" may need to be defined. Do these terms mean the library cannot charge the patron for access? Or do they mean that the use of content for purposes of a possible successful patent application is not permissible?

Note that if you are licensing certain content for use on your Web site, such as an image for your home page, you should ensure that the license allows this particular use. In fact, this may be a useful negotiating point. For instance, if the content owner asks for $1,000 for the use of his or her image on your home page and you only have a budget of $200, you may be able to pay $200 for use of the image on a page other than your home page.

USAGE RESTRICTIONS

Licensing Tip: Ensure that any restrictions are fair and reasonable and do not interfere with your intended use of the licensed content.

There may be certain things which the license specifically states are not permissible, that is, things an authorized user or the library may not do with the licensed content. First and foremost, the library may not share the licensed content with any unauthorized users. Other usage restrictions include the following:

- Substantial or systematic copying. (This is to prevent an entire issue or a substantial part of a journal from being copied, including copying one article at a time, and over time, resulting in a copy of an entire journal.)

- Transmitting content, including digital or other reproductions of content, to other than authorized users (i.e., redistribution is not permissible, for example, by redistribution, reselling, or loaning).

- Removing the publisher's copyright notice on any content.[6]

- Modifying or altering the content. (Ensure that this does not conflict with any intended use of the content. If you need to modify the licensed content, for example, for teaching purposes, ensure that this is permitted under the license.)

- Merging, value-adding, or including content with any other product, service, or database, or creating a derivative work.

- Undertaking any activity that may harm the content owner's ability to sell his or her content.

- Using the licensed content in any commercial manner (including selling it for a fee or for a profit).

- Sharing the content in any manner with other libraries or consortiums of libraries or any other unauthorized users.

LICENSE FEE/PAYMENT

Licensing Tip: There is no magic to determining the appropriate license fee. The library must examine the value of the content (to the library), its own budget, the use of the content, and the alternative content. The library must also take into account how the fee will be paid; for example, based upon duration of online use, upon the number of sites from which the content is available, per-use of content, etc.

How will you be paying the licensor for use of the content? Will the licensor be paid per-use of content (e.g., per article), for time the content is accessed, based upon the number of sites from which the content is available, or based on a set fee for a specified period of time with unlimited access during that time? There are no standards for method of payment—it depends on what works for the parties involved.

In determining the appropriate fee, both content owners and libraries must be able to determine the value of the electronic content being licensed. As licensing electronic content is still new to most libraries, this may involve some guesswork or experimentation. If you are unable to accurately determine the value of the content being licensed, let the content owner know, and you may be able to arrange an interim deal to help you determine this value.

In addition, libraries have to consider their budget for any product and how flexible this budget may be. For instance, if your library is able to license an online journal subscription for $5,000 for use by all patrons with a library card, can your library afford an additional $1,000 to ensure that all members of the public may equally access the content? In many situations, licenses allow for flexibility in terms and conditions, and such terms and conditions are balanced against payment for using that content.

When you do agree upon a fee, it is in a library's best interest to ensure that it is inclusive, and includes all services relating to accessing the electronic products under the license, as well as all applicable taxes, so that there are no hidden costs at a later stage.

In determining your budget for licensing content, you will have to take into account various factors such as expected use of the content, any maintenance or training costs associated with accessing that content, preferences for formats in which the content may be accessible, whether you need to purchase any additional software or hardware in order to access the content, and future costs for such things as updates to the content, or future license fees for updated or archived content.

It is helpful to understand where the content owner is coming from when putting a price on his content, and you may even want to discuss with him how he is valuing it, so you understand his point of view in your negotiations.

Some factors that the content owner may take into account when putting a price tag on his content are the following:

- The cost, if any, of converting print materials to digital format
- The cost of maintaining the electronic content or database, including updating the information and servicing and maintaining any necessary hardware
- Design costs and packaging
- The costs of developing and maintaining software to access digital content
- The expected volume of usage of the content, if the licensor is providing online access
- The intrinsic value of the content itself (e.g., financial, cultural, aesthetic)
- The medium in which the content is supplied (CD-ROM, digital tape, floppy disk, online access to remote server)
- Expectations of the future need for and value of the information
- The ability to substitute the digital format for hard copies of the content with attendant savings in storage and staff
- Increased ability to search and maintain digital information
- The content owner's savings if the print version is no longer produced or distributed[7]

In addition, some publishers and content owners may be concerned about the loss of advertising revenue which was available in print publications.

You also need to address when the fee is due and payable, whether it is payable in stages, and the amount of each payment. This may all affect how much you are able to pay for the content.

Pricing Models

Payment methods vary from license to license. You must look at all of your particular circumstances to determine which payment method or which combination of them makes the most sense for any particular license.

There are numerous pricing models from which content owners and libraries may choose. In some situations, the content owner/publisher may offer you more than one model to choose from. In other situations, the content owner has only one pricing model to offer you. In some circumstances, the content owner may be open to your suggestions in terms of a new and creative pricing model.

Discussions in setting fees for digital licensing often focus on (*a*) subscription fees for limited or unlimited use, and (*b*) pay-per-use. Even within these two models, there are many variations, some of which are included below.

PAY-PER-USE MODELS

- A set fee for each log-on to the online content
- A set fee for each search of the online content
- A set fee for each download of an article. (Is this a printout or electronic download? This would need to be defined in the agreement.)
- A fee per length of online time
- A fee per search

SUBSCRIPTION MODELS

- Subscription fees (annual, quarterly, monthly, or otherwise) for unlimited use (i.e., allowing concurrent/simultaneous use for any quantity of content)

    The number of concurrent users may need to be defined (e.g., allowing five users to access the content at the same time)

- Subscription fees for limited use

    Based on a set number of users, or size of institution

    Based on the number of pages downloaded

    Based on the number of workstations or computers in the library (i.e., no remote access. If the library occupies more than one physical location, this would need to be addressed in the license.)

OTHER MODELS

Any model that the library and content owner agree upon is feasible. Such other models include:

- Initial fees for installation of software and any special hardware and no subsequent fees (though no fee for software seems to be the norm)

- Cost of print journal plus a percent for electronic access
- Cost of print journal plus a set fee for online access based on the number of workstations in a library
- No fee for using a limited amount of the data as a "teaser/promotional" tool in order to encourage subscriptions for the entire database
- No fee for "looking" and only a fee for downloading, or for printing (and can charge at a variety of rates for either or both)
- Fee for unlimited intranet use
- Fee for "value-added" resellers/republisher; different fee for those who do not enhance the content

TWO SUBSCRIPTION MODELS COMPARED

Each pricing model has its advantages and disadvantages. The following comparison discusses the strengths and weaknesses of two different subscription models. It may be helpful for your library to go through a similar analysis to determine what may make sense for you.

Subscription fees (annual) for unlimited use; i.e., allowing concurrent/simultaneous use for any quantity of permitted uses.

> *Advantages:* This model allows for less administration, since there is only one set payment per payment period (year). It may be easier for libraries to budget this set amount. Less record-keeping and monitoring are required to determine, for instance, how many pages are downloaded by a library and its patrons.

> *Disadvantages:* This model makes it difficult for the publisher to determine the value of his content, since he may not have actual knowledge of statistics concerning the use of electronic content (though record-keeping could be built into it). The model may not be ideal in the initial stages of licensing content, though it may be preferable after benefiting from statistical information. Also, it may be harder to monitor who is accessing the content and whether they are covered by the license. Fewer libraries may be interested in licensing content if their patrons can obtain access through "broad" licenses such as this at other libraries.

Subscription fees for limited use; i.e., for a set number of users or number of page downloads.

> *Advantages:* This model is more accurate for publishers and libraries who wish to determine the value of the content by knowing how much is being downloaded. The publisher may be required to provide a simple means for automatically recording searches of licensed contents; some libraries may insist that this means be the publisher's responsibility.

> *Disadvantages:* Libraries may not always have the amount of access required to meet the demands of their patrons. There is a burden on libraries to keep records (and on the publisher to ensure record-keeping is accurate). There are burdens in terms of both administration and costs. Libraries will need to set up some sort of workstation registration or authentication to ensure that only authorized users are accessing the content. Alternatively, the publisher may have to ensure that only certain IP (Internet Protocol) addresses have access to the content.

OTHER CONSIDERATIONS

A further point is whether the license fee is all-inclusive or whether other services and products are subject to an additional fee. What about applicable taxes? It is best to make this clear so that the library knows exactly what it is getting for the fee.

The license should also address when the license fee is due. Is it due upon signing of the agreement or is it due at a later date? Or is the fee payable in stages, and if so, what is the frequency and amount of each payment? It is common to attach these details in an appendix to the agreement.

Notwithstanding the price models offered to your library, it is possible that special arrangements may be made with the content owner on a case-by-case basis. For example, if you are a virtual or digital library, you may be able to negotiate a different pricing scheme. The same is true for libraries that are part of a consortium (i.e., a collective subscription by a group of libraries).

LICENSOR OBLIGATIONS

> **Licensing Tip:** Ensure that the licensor's obligations allow you continuous access to the licensed content, and include safeguards to ensure that downtime will be limited.

This clause sets out what the licensor is obliged to do under the agreement. The licensor's key obligation is to provide you with the content. Some licenses merely state this obligation. Some licenses incorporate these obligations into other clauses in the license. Additional issues that it would be helpful to include in your license are the following:

What format will the information be provided to you; i.e., CD-ROM, DVD, digital tape, or some other physical form, or online via the licensor's server, or through a network, or by a file transfer such as FTP (File Transfer Protocol)?

If you are receiving a CD-ROM, will it be in working order and free of defects?

If you are accessing the owner's server, what about server problems? Does the licensor agree to take adequate steps to ensure that service interruptions are as infrequent as possible? Will there be backup servers? Can the hardware handle a minimum number of simultaneous users? Does the license specify the quantity of downtime that is unacceptable? Does the license state that the subscription fees will be adjusted or rebates given if there are frequent service interruptions?

However you access the content, will the content owner provide technical support? (See also the section "Support and Documentation.")

How often will the content be updated? Monthly? Weekly?

Will you be notified of changes to content? If so, how will you be notified?

It is important that your agreement address in what format the content will be supplied to you, when it will be supplied, and what technical or other support you will receive in the event that there is a problem accessing the information. It is generally not possible to ask for totally uninterrupted access when accessing content from the licensor's server, but you should ask for reasonable efforts from the content owner and specify that a certain amount of interruptions results in a rebate of fees to you. If possible, it is helpful that you are notified before downtime for service or updates, that routine servicing of the server be done during off-peak hours, and that explanations or notices for downtime are sent as soon as possible.

DELIVERY AND CONTINUING ACCESS
TO THE LICENSED CONTENT

Licensing Tip: Specifics as to the delivery of the content will secure maximum use of the content by the library.

Ask the publisher about the history of the content being licensed, how often it is updated, added to, and detracted from. In order for the library to derive maximum benefit from the licensed content, include a date of delivery of the content or when the library may access the content itself, the frequency of delivery (assuming the content is changing, being updated, etc.), and the format. Before signing an agreement, sample the content and ensure its technology is compatible with yours and that the content is in a format and medium that your library and patrons may easily access, or work toward remedying this prior to the effective date of the license. Generally, if the content is not available on time, the publisher will have a specific amount of time, e.g., thirty days, to remedy this situation. (This is addressed in the section "Termination" below.) This clause may also discuss other technological details of accessing the content.

If you are subscribing to electronic content that is also available in print form, you may wish to include a clause stating which format will be available first, and the time difference between the delivery of two formats.

You should address the situation of the publisher or content owner's discontinuing publication of some of the content being licensed. When specified content is no longer available during the duration of the license, your license should state that you are entitled to a proportionate amount of your fee to be reimbursed. You may be more exact and state something to the effect that if more than 10 percent of the content is no longer available, then you are entitled to a 10 percent reimbursement of fees paid or payable.

SUPPORT AND DOCUMENTATION

Licensing Tip: Ensure that you have sufficient support or documentation—either for free or for a reasonable fee—to access the licensed content in the necessary manner.

It is helpful for a license to include specifics about the support and assistance available for an electronic product. Ideally, this clause would stipulate that unlimited support is provided at no additional fee. Although unlimited support is ideal, if the publisher does not provide you with this, try to negotiate some free support, another level of low-cost support, and perhaps an annual support plan for an annual fee or per enquiry. Support may include a telephone support HelpDesk (and the license should state the telephone number and if it is toll-free); and online help either through a searchable list of questions and answers on the content owner's Web site, or through real-time online support in which you may e-mail a support person. Further, your license may address the hours of operation of support (e.g., 24/7 or during business hours EST) and the amount of time you may have to wait to obtain support (i.e., through a telephone or in response to an e-mail). In some situations, the library may want its patrons to also have access to support.

Documentation in the form of a user's manual may also be helpful in using the licensed content efficiently. And ask the content owner whether there is ongoing documentation such as a print or e-mail newsletter.

LIBRARY/LICENSEE OBLIGATIONS

> **Licensing Tip:** Your obligations should be reasonable and not overly burdensome; for the most part, they should comply with the current day-to-day operations of your library.

As a user of content, you have certain obligations toward the owner of the content. Your main obligation is to use the content according to the terms and conditions set out in the license. The content owner may want to place specific restrictions on how its content may be used in your library. Here are some examples of library obligations you may see in a license offered to you:

- You will notify your patrons or authorized users about the terms and conditions of the license, including any limitations on the use of the licensed content.
- You will only use the content in the manner set out in the license and will not otherwise use that content in a copyright manner without prior permission from the content owner.
- You will be required to monitor illegal uses of the content. (Generally, you should not be obligated to police illegal uses, but perhaps to inform the licensor of any illegal uses that you may spot.)
- You agree to cooperate in the implementation of any security and control procedures relating to accessing the licensed content (for example, issuing passwords to authorized users).

You must keep statistics regarding the usage of the content. (See below in the section "Monitoring Use.")

Because of the ease of copying and distributing electronic content, content owners are concerned about uses beyond their control and try to protect themselves as much as possible. This is because once a library patron accesses licensed content, the publisher has no contractual remedies against a library patron who uses it in an unauthorized manner (because the license is between the library and publisher and cannot be enforced against the patron). However, the publisher may have other remedies under the copyright laws of the country where the content is being used.[8] Practically speaking, a content owner does not want to be in the position of having to enforce its rights against individual users of its content. Does this mean that license agreements should obligate libraries to be responsible for the use of content by their sublicensees or patrons? Many argue that this is an unreasonable request and burden to put upon libraries. Libraries are always advised to stay away from policing activities.

A compromise is for the library to be responsible for acts that are within its direct control or within "reasonable" control. However, a library may argue that it is impossible to monitor even authorized users and may request that its obligations be met if it does certain things. (See the list of suggested safeguards below.) One possibility is that a library's responsibility extend so far as to inform its own legal counsel or the content owner if the library sees anything that may appear to be an infringement, and that it cooperate with the content owner to stop further infringements. A library should not be in the position of interpreting copyright law and determining what uses may constitute an infringement of copyright.

Some safeguards may be employed by libraries to help prevent patrons from infringement of copyright, and these may be included in a license. These safeguards may obligate libraries to do certain things such as:

Each reproduced article should state the content owner's name and e-mail address, along with a copyright notice or warning (as agreed upon).

Wherever and whenever access to the licensed content is made available, patrons and researchers should be explicitly warned about copyright law and license agreements. For example, a copyright notice should be posted near a computer terminal. Where access is remote, a copyright notice should appear prior to granting access to the content. The wording of such a notice would be agreed upon in advance by the content owner and the library.

The library should make information on copyright law and license agreements easily accessible to patrons, for instance, via its own Web site, as a listing of links to other Web sites, or on a shelf in the library.

In addition, it is important that all librarians and library staff are made fully aware of the license terms and conditions and may easily access them should it be necessary to clarify which conditions apply to which license and content. (See the section on "Managing Multiple Licenses" in chapter 8.)

MONITORING USE

> **Licensing Tip:** Take great caution in agreeing to monitor any use of the licensed content. Ensure that your library has safeguards if you are required to do so.

The licensor may require your library to take security precautions, such as requiring passwords for use of the licensed content, in order to ensure that the content is used under the terms and conditions set out in the license. The licensor may also want your library to track usage of its content. Although it is not unreasonable to take security precautions, do not guarantee the licensor that you can prevent unauthorized use of the content by your patrons. This is something that you cannot prevent no matter how effective your security precautions are. It is acceptable to agree to have security precautions in place, as discussed in the preceding section, but do not promise that you will prevent all unauthorized use of the licensor's content.

The licensor may also want your library to track usage of its content— who is using the content, how often it is being used. Tracking usage raises the question of privacy. Monitoring how and when your patrons are using licensed content may be an invasion of their privacy. It also requires staff time and equipment, such as software and even hardware, to conduct this monitoring. Before agreeing to track usage, think about the privacy of your patrons and the other costs involved for your library. If you do agree to track usage, it is a good idea to inform your patrons about this practice.

MORAL RIGHTS

> **Licensing Tip:** If your library is using an individual person's content on your Web site, you may want to obtain a waiver of moral rights at least in those countries where a waiver is permis-

sible (and be sure to word it this way so that you do not have to name specific countries where a waiver is permitted).

Moral rights is one of those lesser-known areas of copyright law that is gaining exposure with global licensing, i.e., the licensing of content on the Internet. Although moral rights exist in many countries, they do so on a varying degree. For instance, in the European Union countries, there are strong and perpetual moral rights provisions in the copyright statutes. In the United States, moral rights are much more limited. In Canada and the United Kingdom, moral rights are fairly strong but are lessened by the fact that they may be waived by the authors of copyright works and expire when the duration of copyright expires.

What are moral rights? Moral rights protect the reputation of the author of a work and not necessarily the owner of a work. For instance, a painter would be protected by moral rights if someone modified the painting by adding a moustache to the face of one of the persons in the painting, provided this would harm the reputation of the painter. Moral rights also ensure that the author has his or her name associated with the work, may use a pseudonym, or may remain anonymous.

Depending on how a library is using content, it may need to address the issue of moral rights. In general, most online subscription or database agreements do not include a clause dealing with moral rights. However, if your library is specifically including content on its Web site, then you may need to address this issue.

CREDITS

Licensing Tip: Ensure that the credits are not in a position or in a size that interferes with the enjoyment of the content.

The license may specifically state how any licensed content will include the content owner's name and copyright notice. Generally, the content owner will want its name, the copyright symbol, and the year of publication on the licensed content. This way, anyone who has access to the content through the library is made aware that the content is protected by copyright and knows the name of the owner of the copyright. Some licenses go further and state where the notice will be placed and the size of the notice.[9]

Related to credits may be the issue of content owners listing licensees on their Web site. For instance, Publisher X may list Library C as a licensee. If the content owner wishes to do this, he should have permission from the library. For various reasons, this is something to which a library may not wish to agree.

TERRITORY

> **Licensing Tip:** Worldwide rights will cost your library much more than narrow rights such as U.S. rights, so you may be able to negotiate a lower payment if you can narrow the territories for the rights you want to license.

The word "territory" refers to the geographic boundary of the license. For example, content may be licensed for use only in a specific state or province, or a country, or sometimes the license may refer to North America. Global or worldwide rights are the norm for online products, since it is difficult and not always feasible to distinguish territories on the Internet, but stand-alone products such as CD-ROMs or DVDs may be licensed by specific territories. If your library is based in the United States and you have patrons accessing your library from outside the country, you will need to address this in your license. See further discussion of this issue in the sections "Authorized Users" and "Authorized Site" below. In fact, you may not need a specific clause for territory if these other clauses address the same issues. Sometimes "territory" is defined in the definitions section of the license.

AUTHORIZED USERS

> **Licensing Tip:** Determine and set out in the license who will be using the licensed content. Define this as broadly as possible in order to ensure that any relevant persons are included and you do not have to obtain further permission from the content owner for other users.

It is important to determine in your license who is authorized to use the licensed content. How will authorized users be defined? Will certain patrons of the library and library staff be excluded? What about the public: will they be authorized to use the content?

The content owner may want to limit who may access the content and where (see the section "Authorized Site" below). It is important to ensure that this part of the agreement is broad enough to serve all of your patrons and your staff, and the public if necessary.

Many agreements use the term "authorized user" to refer to a sublicensee such as a library patron.

Some authorized users you may want in your agreement include:

- Library employees or staff
- Consultants or independent contractors
- Affiliated researchers
- Specific "registered" persons
- Students (part- and full-time)
- The public. This term would include patrons not specifically affiliated with the library or the institution that runs the library, and who are not physically present on a day-to-day basis at the library, and are often referred to as "walk-ins."

In an academic setting, an authorized user may include library employees, faculty or department members (permanent, temporary, contract, and visiting), staff, consultants, students (part- and full-time) associated with the school, and authorized patrons of the school's library—this could be for in-library or on-the-premises uses as opposed to remote access. Alumni will not automatically be included as authorized users in an academic library setting; this is something you may wish to negotiate if you want alumni to have access to the licensed content. In some situations, students enrolled in a specific course may be specified as an authorized user group.

An important issue to consider is whether the public may be an authorized user (if so, this may be reflected in the license fee).

Another consideration is whether the group of authorized users is defined geographically, for instance, all faculty on campus X. If your library has more than one branch, you may want to consider a multibranch license so that patrons at other locations can have the same access as patrons at the main library. University libraries want to ensure that all of their campuses are covered by any license agreements. In some situations, your patrons may need to access the licensed content from other countries. If this applies to you, make sure your license allows this and is not limited, for instance, to the United States. See also the discussion in the "Authorized Site" section below.

How will authorized users gain access to the licensed content? Various methods include authenticating users by their Internet Protocol (IP) address, through passwords, electronic keys, or other protocols agreed upon between the library and content owner.

See also the discussion in the "Sublicenses" section of this chapter.

AUTHORIZED SITE

Licensing Tip: Ensure that any access limitations still allow for the reasonable use of the content by your patrons, and contemplate any off-site access that you may need in your license.

It is important to specify from where the authorized users may access the content. Generally, this relates to two places, on-site (i.e., on the premises of the library), and remotely (i.e., from a home or office or while traveling or living in a different city, state, or country). On-site access may be easier to control, and content owners may be better able to ensure some degree of compliance with the license agreement. However, libraries often require remote access, depending on how patrons access or use their facilities and network. For instance, if you provide proxy server access to authorized users, this access will be available from anywhere in the world. If this applies to your patrons, ensure that your license addresses this fact. If many of your institution's patrons travel and access content from outside your country, ensure that the license allows for access by them. In fact, you may prefer to have a license that is non-site specific. More simply, if the users of the licensed content need to access that content at home or from their offices, this should be expressly permitted in the license.

In addition, your license may need to set out whether access will be permitted from a single computer, or from a network with a specified number of simultaneous/concurrent users, or perhaps an unlimited number of users.

You will need to be specific in the license about who authorized users are and what site access is authorized. Never assume that unnamed users or sites are included under the license.

COPYRIGHT OWNERSHIP

Licensing Tip: Throughout the licensing process, keep in mind that you are licensing the content and not obtaining any assignment or permanent rights in it.

Often the license will state who the copyright owner is of the electronic content, and of the print content, if there is any. Some licenses may state something to the effect that copyright remains with the content owner and that the library has the right to use the content (without transfer of copyright ownership) under the terms and conditions of the license. As discussed in chapter 3, a license is merely a permission to use copyright work and is not an assignment or transfer of those rights. Remember that you are licensing the use of, or access to, specific digital content, and you do not need to own copyright in that content in order to access and use it under the terms and conditions of your license.

Also, you want to ensure that the publisher does in fact have the rights in the content that it is licensing to you. This does not necessarily mean ownership rights, as long as the licensor has the rights to license you the content. This is further discussed below in the sections "Warranties" and "Indemnity and Limitation of Liability."

DURATION OF GRANT OF RIGHTS (TERM OF AGREEMENT)

Licensing Tip: By agreeing to a shorter duration of the grant of rights, you may lower the license fee for use of the content.

"Duration" or "term of agreement" relates to the period of time in which the license persists, or in which the publisher or content owner provides access to its content. The license may only be canceled before the end of the term if there is a fundamental breach of the agreement or if a provision in the agreement allows for early termination upon the occurrence of a certain event.

The duration may be based on a specific length of time (e.g., from January 1, 2002, to December 31, 2002, or for one year from the signing of the license), or it may be based upon the payment of each yearly subscription fee. Educational institutions may prefer that the license cover the school year as opposed to the calendar year or another designation of time. It is important to specify how long the agreement continues. The agreement can specify a certain date on which it will terminate or a certain length of time for which it will continue. It is also possible that the agreement renew automatically under the same conditions and terms, by inserting a renewal clause in the agreement (see the "Renewal" section below). This would take place provided that both parties to the agreement are satisfied with it and would like it to automatically renew.

The agreement should address how and when the agreement can be terminated. You can include the right to terminate the agreement for serious violations of the terms and conditions in the agreement, or include termination of the agreement for any reason, provided notice is given to the other party. Automatic termination is another option, whereby you set forth in the agreement what events automatically end the agreement. Examples include default in payment, bankruptcy, or material breach for invoking automatic termination of the agreement.

RENEWAL

> **Licensing Tip:** Consider an automatic renewal clause that allows your library to continue a satisfying licensing arrangement. Make sure your library keeps a careful record that the license will automatically renew unless you notify the publisher in advance.

At the end of the time specified in the contract the contract ends, unless it allows for automatic renewal. You may request a specified period of time of notification should the renewal be at a new price, so the library has time to evaluate that price and determine whether its budget allows for it. For instance, you may request a clause stating that sixty or ninety days' notice prior to the termination of the agreement must be given to you to examine any price increases.

An automatic renewal clause is very inviting in many circumstances, since it means that if both parties are happy with the agreement, then it will continue and you thus do not need to renegotiate the license. If either party is unhappy with the license, then either party may terminate or initiate to renegotiate the license. However, keep in mind that if you do nothing, then the agreement will automatically renew.

Automatic renewal may occur upon certain things happening, such as the payment of a yearly fee, or an increased fee from the previous year. If there is an increased fee, ensure at the time of signing the original agreement that the amount is reasonable and within your budget. Alternatively, an agreement based, for example, on a two-year period could automatically renew for another two years unless one party notifies the other party within a certain number of days prior to expiration of the agreement.

If there is an automatic renewal clause in your license, both the publisher and the library should have the right to terminate the agreement and to halt the automatic renewal; this right should not just benefit the publisher. It is also helpful if the publisher is obligated to notify you that the automatic renewal is about to occur unless you otherwise notify the publisher. However, few publishers would agree to do so. Thus, the managing of your multiple licenses becomes even more important so that you do not continue in automatic licensing arrangements without being aware of doing so.

Where automatic renewal is not included in the license, ask the publisher to notify you several weeks prior to the termination of the license so that you may renew. Although a publisher may resist including this in a license, it is in his best interest to undertake this task to ensure continuing your license with him. Publishers often resist sending out such notices because of the numbers of libraries they would have to notify. If you are part of a consortium license, it is the administrator of the consortium who will be notified prior to automatic renewal.

Without an automatic renewal clause, the license may only be renewed through a new license agreement signed by both parties.

TERMINATION

Licensing Tip: If your license terminates prior to the duration set out in the license, ensure that you are entitled to a refund of your license fees for that period of early termination.

The license will terminate or end when the duration of the license expires, provided there is no automatic renewal of the license.

Generally, the termination clause allows either party to terminate the agreement for a substantial or material breach of the license. For example, a breach would occur in cases where access to the content is no longer available or payment by the library has not been made. Terminating the license must usually be done in writing. Either party should be able to terminate the license for a fundamental breach, and not just the publisher.

It is important that the license should not expire early due to problematic uses of the content by patrons. Although you may take reasonable steps to inform your patrons of the authorized uses of the content, you should not agree to early termination of the license should this be a problem.

In some situations, a license will end before the expiration of the agreement if there is a fundamental breach of it, that is, if one party does not live up to its obligations. Even in those circumstances, an agreement may provide for a period of thirty days, for example, for the defaulting party to remedy the situation and thus avoid the termination of the agreement. This also ensures that a library does not suddenly lose its access. Most publishers would only agree to such a clause if the library continues to observe the other clauses set out in the agreement relating to such things as usage, modifications, and security.

A publisher should not be able to terminate the license because it has changed the content being licensed. The content should be available as it is described in the license throughout the duration of the agreement. Occasionally, there may be events beyond the publisher's control, such as loss of a content or database supplier, which could trigger such a clause.

A library may want to ensure that should early termination occur due to a breach by the content owner, the library receives a pro rata refund that it has paid for access to that content. Upon early termination, the publisher may request that the content be returned (if feasible) or destroyed.

In addition, there might be a specific provision in the agreement that allows for an earlier termination, for example, upon insolvency, or if one party gives notice to the other party.

PERPETUAL ACCESS/ARCHIVE

> **Licensing Tip:** Discuss with the content owner if and how he may provide ongoing access to previously licensed content ("previously" refers to content paid for but for which the license has expired).

One of the more unsettling issues in relation to libraries licensing digital content is perpetual or ongoing access to the content after the expiration of the license. When your library purchases a print book, you have access to that book indefinitely or at least until it is damaged or worn out. Your purchase of that print book is not on a limited basis; you own the physical book forever. However, when you license digital content, you only have a limited time access to that content. If you license a digital journal and also subscribe to the print journal, then this is less of an issue, since your print journal will form part of your print archives even after your license to the digital content expires.

Different agreements deal with perpetual access in different ways. Some licenses do not address this issue at all. Some provide that the publisher will provide continuing access at its discretion. Some provide access to previous volumes of a publication although the library subscribes only to the current volume. Some provide access to the licensed content "for as long as is practicable" or may even supply the archival content on a CD-ROM. Another route is to provide continuous access to any licensed content under the terms and conditions of the original license.

Depending on what you negotiate, you may need to keep in mind that there will be a cost for you to keep your own archives of electronic content. There may be an initial cost of creating the archive and backing-up the content. There may also be the cost of "renewing data," that is, keeping it in a current and accessible format, or constantly upgrading it to keep up with technological change, which may be relatively expensive. In fact, making your own print copy on acid-free paper may prove more economical than keeping an electronic archive, and may meet your collections needs equally well. Again, if this is something you contemplate, ensure that it is dealt with in your license and you have permission to do this. Being creative in your arrangements will be easier with a solid "licensing needs assessment" you have completed before you begin the license negotiations (see chapter 2).

DISCLAIMERS

> **Licensing Tip:** Ensure that the publisher is not disclaiming or limiting its liability to such an extent that the library is losing necessary protection under the license.

The content owner may include certain disclaimers, for example, that he or she does not warrant that the content will be accessible in any particular hardware or via any particular computer software. The content owner may also stipulate that he or she does not warrant the accuracy or completeness of any information contained in the content, or its merchantability or fitness for a particular purpose. Generally, the publisher (though not individual content owners) will make all reasonable efforts to ensure its server is available to the library on a 24/7 basis, excluding normal network administration and system downtime, and will limit its liability to restoring access. Some disclaimer clause will limit the publisher's liability to no more than the license fee paid—this is something you may wish to discuss with your institution's attorney. Certain publicly funded institutions in the United States are not permitted to sign agreements with a limitation of liability, and you may want to check this with your institution.

WARRANTIES

Licensing Tip: Ensure that the content owner has all the necessary rights to license the content to you and that there are no substantial limitations on these rights.

Warranties are promises that either party makes to the other one in the agreement. For example, the licensor may warrant that he has not infringed the intellectual property rights or other rights of a third party when providing your library with the content. The licensor may also warrant that he has the authority to enter into the contract and to license the content to you, and that this does not conflict with any other licenses entered into by him. If any of the warranties are untrue, then the licensor making the warranty may be subject to certain "penalties" or indemnities, as discussed below.

Often, the warranties and indemnity are set out in the same paragraph in the license.

In general, a library wants a warranty that the content owner is the owner of the electronic works being licensed or has the rights to license them to the library. Otherwise, the library could be paying a license fee to the inappropriate party and may have to pay an additional fee or encounter a copyright infringement suit from the rights holder. Make sure that the warranty is straightforward and unambiguous. Wording like "to the best of the publisher's knowledge" is not acceptable. If the publisher cannot guarantee that it can license the content to you, seek a publisher who can. This warranty should endure for at least the duration of the license, i.e., so that the publisher has the right to license the content throughout the duration of the license.

Although it is not frequently seen, it may be helpful to include a clause that the content owner warrants that he will continue to have the rights being licensed throughout the duration, and any renewals, of the license agreement.

INDEMNITY AND LIMITATION OF LIABILITY

Licensing Tip: Your license should include an indemnity that is strong enough to back up its warranties and to ensure you are compensated should you run into certain legal or other problems. However, the indemnity clause is only as useful as the financial viability of the content owner, and caution should be taken in relying on the indemnity clause.

Often warranties and indemnities are coupled. Whereas the warranty "guarantees" the rights, the indemnity provides for financial compensation should the warranty be false. An indemnity clause states that the licensor must pay the cost of any legal expenses and other claims that arise from breaching the warranties in the agreement. If there is any infringement of rights by the content owner, the indemnity would say something to the effect that the content owner will indemnify the library against "all loss, damage, award, penalties, injuries, costs, claims, and expenses, including reasonable attorney fees, arising out of any actual or alleged infringement." A publisher would prefer a clause in which the indemnity is limited to any actual infringement, as opposed to including any alleged infringements. More generally, a limitation of liability clause sets out how much and what kind of damages the licensor will pay for. The licensor will want to limit its liability by restricting the amount of damages and excluding certain kinds of damages and harms. Many public institutions in the United States may not accept certain limitations of liability in the indemnity, and you may need to check your institution's position on this.

An indemnity is only as useful as the pocketbook of the content owner. In other words, if the content owner cannot pay the amounts set out in the indemnity, then the indemnity becomes useless. You may wish to investigate the financial viability of the content owner when considering licensing content from him and determine what sort of indemnity clause makes sense for you in the circumstances.

It is easy to go overboard when asking for warranties and indemnities. It is not reasonable for either party to ask for or to provide an ironclad warranty-indemnity that is not critical to the licensing and necessary use of the licensed content.

NOTES

1. Some do not believe that permission to include a link to a site is necessary. In the United States, legal cases settled out of court suggest that a link to the home page of a site is less likely to cause a legal problem than a deep link to an internal page of a site.
2. This does not seem to be done very often. Usually the content is accessible from the publisher's server.
3. This may not be necessary if the content is delivered online from the publisher.
4. Fair use is a concept in the U.S. Copyright Act. Fair dealing is a comparable though generally narrower concept found in the copyright statutes of Canada, Australia, the United Kingdom, and several other countries.
5. This is not a legal opinion, and legal advice should be sought should this be an issue.

6. This may be an infringement of the U.S. Digital Millennium Copyright Act. See chapter 3.

7. This list is from the library's perspective as found at the Yale University Library LibLicense site at http://www.library.yale.edu/~llicense/paygen.shtml.

8. This is according to international copyright law principles, primarily the Berne Convention (http://www.wipo.int). Courts apply the copyright laws of the country in which the alleged unauthorized use takes place.

9. Omitting or removing such copyright management information may be an infringement of the U.S. Digital Millennium Copyright Act. See chapter 3.

FURTHER CLAUSES

This chapter has set out major clauses and some minor ones that you are likely to encounter and want addressed in your licenses. Consider which ones may work for you and how to ensure they are part of your license. You may also want to consider certain standard clauses that are discussed in chapter 5 and are referred to as "boilerplates."

Boilerplate Clauses

*There are only two kinds of people
who are really fascinating—people
who know absolutely everything,
and people who know absolutely nothing.*

—Oscar Wilde

COMMON BOILERPLATE CLAUSES

Standard form provisions, commonly referred to as "boilerplates," are general contract provisions that appear in many different types of agreements, and not necessarily just in license agreements. A number of boilerplates will be part of any license agreement. Listed and discussed below are common ones you are likely to see in the license agreements with which you are dealing.

- Alternative Dispute Resolution
- Amendments
- Binding Effect
- Confidential Information
- Currency
- Entire Agreement
- Force Majeure
- Governing Law
- Independent Parties
- Interpretation
- Notice
- Remedies
- Severability
- Signature
- Survival
- Transferability or Assignment
- Waiver

ALTERNATIVE DISPUTE RESOLUTION

Licensing Tip: Including an alternative dispute resolution clause in your license may be a quicker and less expensive way to resolve any disputes arising from the license and will benefit both parties.

Disputes or ambiguities relating to an agreement may be settled by a number of mechanisms including a court of law, arbitration, mediation, and negotiation. The general trend in North America in many types of agreements is to include an arbitration clause, also called an alternative dispute resolution (ADR) clause. Compared to resorting to court and court proceedings, arbitration can be a less expensive and much quicker way to resolve a dispute arising under your agreement.

Generally, the license should state that the parties will try in good faith to resolve any disputes arising from the license and to resort to negotiation, mediation, and then, if necessary, arbitration. Arbitration still involves considerable expense in the United States, since arbitrators are usually chosen through the American Arbitration Association (www.adr.org). That is why licenses often allow for negotiation, and then mediation, prior to resorting to arbitration.

An arbitration clause may state that the arbitrator be appointed under, and subject to, the arbitration laws in any jurisdiction, should such laws exist. The arbitrator is a neutral third party who renders a decision on behalf of the parties. Arbitration may be binding or nonbinding. "Nonbinding arbitration" means that you may still go to court to resolve this issue, notwithstanding the arbitration process.

Often the ADR clause will state that the costs for ADR will be borne equally by the two parties. Also, these clauses often state that should an in-person meeting be necessary, that it be in a place halfway between the geographical locations of the two parties.

AMENDMENTS

Licensing Tip: Ensure that either party may amend the agreement in writing.

The amendment clause states how the agreement may be modified, i.e., in writing, and signed by both parties who signed the original license agreement. This will ensure that no changes are made to the contract without agreement between the parties. It also emphasizes the point that the only understandings in relation to the licensed content are those agreed to in writing in the original written license or in a written amendment to it. It is only reasonable to have an amendment clause that allows either party to amend the agreement and not just one of the parties.

BINDING EFFECT

Licensing Tip: It may be helpful if the license extends not only to the library but to its successors and assignees.

This clause would allow the license agreement to benefit successors, administrators, heirs (if the licensee is a private library), affiliates, and assigns of the parties signing the license. Usually, the assigns are subject to the prior written approval of the licensor.

CONFIDENTIAL INFORMATION

Licensing Tip: You may wish to keep your business practices confidential by adding a confidentiality clause in your license. However, if you want to be able to share the payment of the license fee with others, exclude the fee as being subject to this confidentiality clause.

In certain circumstances, both content owners and libraries may want certain aspects relating to an agreement to be kept confidential from their competitors and customers. For example, the content owner may want the amount of the license fee kept confidential, and the library may want to keep the usage and names of the users of the licensed content confidential. Each party may want to keep confidential the business and operation practices within its own organization. What remains confidential is a matter of agreement between the content owner and the library, and whatever this information is, the agreement should clearly specify what is to remain confidential and the confidentiality clause should be limited to that information only.

If your institution or library is operated by the U.S. government and is subject to the U.S. Freedom of Information Act or other equivalent legislation, you should not agree to keep the terms of the agreement confidential. Also, if you are a public institution, it is likely that any document created is a public document and may not be subject to confidentiality. Note that although the agreement is a public document, any user statistics are not part of the agreement and you may request that those be kept confidential.

CURRENCY

Licensing Tip: Include the national currency to be used whenever dollar amounts are set out in the license.

Digital licenses are often between content owners and libraries in different countries. For example, a content owner may be based in Canada and the library in the United States. In such a situation, would your license fee be in U.S. or Canadian dollars? This is a matter for the content owner and the library to agree upon. You should always state the currency of the licensing fee and any other dollar amounts set out in the license. For clarity, even if both parties to the license are in the same country, it is helpful to set out the currency of any dollar amounts.

ENTIRE AGREEMENT

Licensing Tip: Make sure that any points you want included in the license are included in the written license and do not rely upon any oral promises or e-mails, etc., to form part of your license.

This clause states that the agreement, along with any appendixes and attachments, stands on its own and represents the entire agreement between the parties. The agreement therefore supersedes any other written or oral agreements and any implied or explicit previous agreements. In other words, any prior e-mails, faxes, telephone conversations, etc., are not part of the agreement. As a practical matter, this means that anything you or the other party has asked for, or agreed to, must be in the written license; otherwise, it will not form part of the agreement.

To be prudent, if a content owner says to you during negotiations not to worry about a specific clause in the agreement because it will not be enforced, you should insist that that clause be removed. Otherwise, it does form part of the agreement, and the other party's promise not to enforce it may itself be unenforceable.

FORCE MAJEURE

Licensing Tip: Ensure that your force majeure clause does not unreasonably include technical difficulties that prevent you from accessing the licensed content.

A force majeure is a condition beyond the control of either party. It literally means "greater force." A force majeure clause excuses a party from performing its obligations under the agreement if there is some unforeseen event beyond the control of that party. This clause applies provided due care could not have been exercised to avoid the failure to perform the obligations in the agreement.

Until recently, force majeure included war, strikes, floods, and other events or conditions that could not be contemplated in advance by either party and that would prevent compliance with the terms and conditions in an agreement. In such circumstances, the contract would not be considered breached and would continue in effect. Regarding license agreements, it is important to include additional conditions in a force majeure clause such as power failures, destruction of network facilities, etc. This is an area where you may wish to consult with your technical experts. Generally, such things as server failures, software bugs, and disputes with copyright owners are not considered to be a force majeure.

A force majeure clause should apply equally to the licensor and licensee.

GOVERNING LAW

Licensing Tip: It is best to choose the governing law, court for submitting a claim, and place of litigation within the state or province and country in which your institution resides, although this is not always negotiable.

Online content generally means global access, and it is very important to specify in any license agreement (*a*) the jurisdiction of law for the interpretation of the license, (*b*) the court for submitting a claim against the other party, and (*c*) the place of litigation.

It is best to choose a jurisdiction with which you are familiar, e.g., your own state or province and country. Any party to an agreement will want that agreement interpreted according to the laws of its own jurisdiction, since each party and its attorneys will be most familiar with those laws. You should specify the state or province under which the agreement will be interpreted, as well as the country. This is because some legal matters, such as contractual ones, are regulated by your state or province, whereas others such as copyright matters are regulated primarily by federal or national laws. Also, your license should set out the state or province in which any legal action or proceeding would be instituted.

In the United States, if your library is part of a state institution, you may be required to have the laws of that state govern your agreement. Be aware of your institution's policies on agreements in general.

The publisher may also have specific reasons for requesting a specific jurisdiction to govern the license.[1] Be creative and be sure to discuss this as part of the negotiations.

An issue related to governing law is that of the place of litigation. Should litigation take place, it can be quite costly if the license states that any litigation or disputes arising from the license should take place in a state or province other than your own. For instance, it would be costly for a Maryland library to litigate in California. You want to choose a jurisdiction that is convenient in order to minimize travel to another state, province, or country should a lawsuit arise.

The governing law clause can be a complicated matter that may need to be discussed with your attorney. Some lawyers may suggest that if you cannot agree upon a jurisdiction, leave it out of the agreement. This is a judgment call that may or may not meet your needs.

INDEPENDENT PARTIES

> **Licensing Tip:** This clause may be more relevant if you are licensing your own library's content than if you are using someone else's content.

This clause would state that the agreement does not create a legal relationship such as a joint venture or partnership between the two parties signing the agreement.

INTERPRETATION

> **Licensing Tip:** This clause ensures that the headings you use in your license will not affect the interpretation of the license.

This clause states that the headings used in the license are for convenience only and are not intended to be part of any interpretations of the license.

NOTICE

> **Licensing Tip:** Carefully specify how notices may be delivered and who the proper recipient is for notices.

This clause states that notices relating to the license (e.g., to prevent an automatic renewal of the license) be in writing. It also specifies how they should be delivered to the other party, e.g., by courier, postal mail, fax, or e-mail. It is important that a contact name for each party is included in this provision so that the correct person receives any notices under this agreement. This will allow for immediate and efficient action on the part of the party receiving the notice.

It is important that the specifics of delivery of the notice are set out in the license; for instance, that the notice should be in writing and delivered by hand, and actual delivery would constitute the time and date of delivery; or if by fax, that a fax back confirming delivery should be sent; or if sent by certified or registered mail, that the notice be deemed to be delivered five days after sending it. In some situations, an e-mail notice may be sufficient, but again this should be clearly set out in the license as to when it is acceptable and how it will be ensured that the recipient actually received the notice.

REMEDIES

Licensing Tip: Include remedies for breach of the license so that each party is aware of what will happen in case the license is breached.

A remedy clause provides for certain remedies in cases where there is a breach of the contract. Examples of remedies include court injunctions to stop an action harming one of the parties to the agreement, and lawsuits to obtain monetary damages. Remedies also include arbitration, as opposed to solving the dispute by way of a court action (see the section "Alternative Dispute Resolution").

SEVERABILITY

Licensing Tip: It is helpful to include a severability clause in case there is a problem with another clause in the license.

This clause states that should any part of the agreement be invalid or unenforceable, that the remaining portions of the agreement, where possible, survive and remain in full force and effect. Some licenses go further and state that only clauses that do not alter the entire licensing arrangement may be severed, and that the entire license should cease should the removal of a clause make it unreasonable to continue the license in a reasonable manner; this reflects the law in many jurisdictions.

SIGNATURE

Licensing Tip: Ensure that only authorized persons sign the license.

It is important that the person who signs the license actually has legal authority to do so. If an unauthorized person at the library signs the license, then either party may later argue that the license is invalid and does not apply to the institution it purports to bind. Some licenses include a clause to the effect that the parties to the license warrant that the signing persons have the authority to bind their institution or company. In a public library, for example, the library board will appoint an authorized signing agent or person. Your library's corporate counsel can help you determine who in your library has authority to bind it to a legal agreement.

The person who signs the license may protect herself by asking her library for written documentation setting out that she does in fact have authority to sign the license. This may protect her should a content owner ever take legal action personally against the signing person.

SURVIVAL

Licensing Tip: Ensure that the survival of any of the specified clauses does not unreasonably obligate you after the license expires.

This clause states that certain clauses survive the termination of the agreement. Generally, clauses that would survive are those relating to warranties and indemnities, but your agreement may specify the survival of any clauses that make sense for your particular circumstances.

TRANSFERABILITY OR ASSIGNMENT

Licensing Tip: Although you may think it is unlikely that your library will require such a clause to apply to it, make sure this clause applies equally to both parties.

If your library is incorporated into another entity, then what happens to the license agreements you have signed? Does the new entity automatically assume them? And what happens if the content owner is purchased by a new content owner—are you still obligated to the terms and conditions in the license with the original content owner? All this depends on what your license sets out. The license may state that it terminates should either of the signing parties cease to exist. Or it may allow the license to be assumed by the new entity, or perhaps only so upon approval by both parties. This approval should be in writing and signed by both parties. If there is an automatic transfer without approval of either party, then you may want to obtain a written promise from the new entity stating that it will fulfill all of the obligations in the license. (If your library is licensing its own content for use by others, carefully consider this question of transferability, since you may want to consider such factors as the reputation of the new company using your content.)

WAIVER

Licensing Tip: If one party ignores the breach of a provision in the license, it does not necessarily mean that this provision is being waived and is no longer part of the agreement.

This clause generally states that if one party fails to enforce any particular clause in the license, this does not mean that the clause is being waived and is then not part of the license. For example, if one party ignores a violation of the license, then not only does the license continue, but the clause that is being violated is not necessarily waived. Generally, what you want to see in such a clause is that the only way that a clause may be waived by either party is by making an amendment to the agreement in writing (see "Amendments").

NOTE

1. One of UCITA's effects may be the increased number of licenses that specify states in which UCITA has passed. At the time of writing, only Maryland and Virginia have passed UCITA. There are opt-in and opt-out provisions in both of these states' UCITA laws, and libraries should not be forced to agree to a jurisdiction in which UCITA is law. See chapter 3 for more information on UCITA.

NEGOTIATING BOILERPLATES

Boilerplates are equally important to other clauses in your license agreement and should not be skimmed over when negotiating, reviewing, or interpreting a license. Read the boilerplate clauses carefully because they vary from agreement to agreement, and make sure that they are fair and reasonable. Ensure that the wording used in the boilerplates reflects your negotiations with the content owner, and fits the needs of your particular circumstances.

Un-Intimidating Negotiations

Your gentleness shall force more than
your force move us to gentleness.

—Shakespeare, *As You Like It*

When I entered into my first contract negotiation, I was scared. To me, negotiation meant fighting and struggling and persuading the other party to meet all my needs. It sounded like an aggressive, argumentative, unpleasant activity that I would rather avoid, given the opportunity. After my first contract negotiation, I completely turned around. I realized it is the word "negotiation" that makes it sound intimidating. The process is about discussing what makes sense to both parties and finding a compromise to satisfy both parties— a win-win situation. With that enlightenment, I now enjoy the whole process.

WHAT DOES "NEGOTIATION" MEAN?

In simple terms, a negotiation is a discussion between at least two parties that leads to an outcome of a certain issue. In digital licensing, it means a discussion between a library and content owner that leads to a set of mutually agreed-upon terms and conditions relating to the use of specific content. The dictionary meaning of "negotiation" is "[m]utual discussions and arrangement of the terms of a transaction or agreement."[1]

UNDERSTANDING TWO PERSPECTIVES

Preparation of your frame of mind is an important initial task in any negotiation. Negotiation is not an "I win-you lose" affair. The content owner and you have the same thing in mind. You both want to enter into a relationship in which the content owner is fairly compensated for the use of his or her content while you have the right to use that content in the manner necessary for your situation, for example, to provide access to patrons, store in a digital form, or distribute by e-mail.

Librarians often feel powerless entering into, and during the process of, negotiating. Content owners like publishers and aggregators seem to have all the money and plenty of potential customers (and therefore power), while librarians often have only limited resources. However, in a negotiation, you are seeking an end result that works for both parties. By developing alternatives and being flexible, you may find that there is a way for both parties to reach their goals.

ARE ALL LICENSES NEGOTIABLE?

There are both negotiable and nonnegotiable licenses. For instance, the licenses that accompany store-bought or online-purchased computer software are usually nonnegotiable. Store-bought software comes with what we call "shrinkwrap" licenses, and online-purchased software comes with "Webwrap" licenses (the license we agree to before downloading software off the Internet). "Nonnegotiable" means that if you do not agree to the terms and conditions of use, then you must either return the software to the distributor, or in the case of online software, you do not download the software.

Nonnegotiable licenses may apply to any type of content, including electronic reports, periodicals, and databases. Although nonnegotiable licenses appear to be non-negotiable, there are many instances where you may be able to change certain terms and conditions in the license. If you are faced with a license that seems nonnegotiable, and you would like to license that particular content, always let the content owner know your position and see whether he or she is willing to discuss alternative terms and conditions of licensing. You may be pleasantly surprised by the outcome!

THREATS DO NOT WORK

You never want to threaten any points and close doors to discussion. However, you may wish to keep at the back of your mind the fact that you are able to access a similar or comparable product from a different content owner or distributor so you do not feel obligated to enter into an agreement that does not work for you.

If you find yourself in a situation where your library cannot live with the demands of the license but you really do want access to that particular content, contact the content owner or distributor and discuss with them the possibility of changing some of the terms and conditions. The best approach would be to say that you really want to enter into a license to access that particular content, but you need some amendments to the license offered to you, otherwise you and your patrons would not be able to fully benefit from the content.

LETTER AND E-MAIL AGREEMENTS

In some situations, an electronic publisher or content owner may have a more casual approach to the licensing of their content. For example, they may send you a letter or e-mail setting out what content is being licensed and how you may use it. Again, this may be negotiable upon communication by you that certain terms and conditions in the letter or e-mail do not meet your needs.

ORAL AGREEMENTS

Although it is infrequent, it is possible that a content owner does not provide you with any written license or documentation setting out how you may use their content. In such a circumstance, you may either request that they put something in writing or alternatively that you or your lawyers draft something for review by the content owner. If the content owner insists on oral permission, send them a fax or mail a letter setting out a summary of your telephone conversation and the agreed-upon terms and conditions of use of the content. That way you will have some record of the conversation should you or another person in your library later need to refer to it. Make sure that your library has a good system in place to track such correspondence.

NEGOTIABLE LICENSES

Certain products like a costly electronic database or an online subscription to a journal may require the negotiation of specific terms and conditions of use to match your needs. Through your discussions and negotiations with the owner of the content (e.g., the publisher of the database or online journal), the owner and yourself will negotiate and agree upon exactly the terms and conditions under which the content can be used. How do you ensure that you obtain the best possible terms and the ones that meet your needs and the needs of your library and its patrons? How do you negotiate to obtain those terms and conditions?

This chapter is written from the perspective of the user or licensee—the one licensing the content of someone else—for example, libraries, schools, and others who negotiate for the use of others' content. However, more and more often (especially in digital media), these same institutions are licensing their own content (e.g., a library may license manuscripts or images it owns for use in someone else's Web site). These same tips are helpful to libraries when they act as "content owners," with some necessary adjustment for approaching the issue from the other perspective.

TIPS ON NEGOTIATIONS

The following are a series of tips for negotiating license agreements. These are divided into two sections: "Before You Begin Negotiations" and "During the Negotiations."

The negotiations may be for licenses with individuals (e.g., a photographer whose image you post on your Web site) or with corporate copyright owners (such as a database provider or electronic publisher).

Before You Begin Negotiations

There are many things you have to consider before beginning your negotiations. Three basic points are:

- Know what you want, need, and can pay for.
- Ask: never make assumptions.
- Try to understand what the content owner's needs and perspective are (and make sure the owner understands yours).

BE PREPARED

Be prepared by having all the information you need. What do you want from the content owner? Know specifically the nature of the content and how you will use it. It is a good idea to talk to others in your workplace to see how certain content will be used—will software be placed on six or eight computers? Will access to the online database be permitted only to staff, or will the general public have access to the database? Will access be permitted off the library's premises, and how about in other states or countries? With the rise of distance education as an alternative method of delivering university education, you may need to take into account the possibility that some of your users may be in other countries. Does the license permit distance-education uses of the licensed content? Who will be using the content, and what will they be doing with this material? Will it be your patrons wanting to download information from your Web site? When negotiating with the copyright holder, discuss who will be allowed to use the material, how it can be used, and what happens in the case of unauthorized use.

What sorts of terms and conditions did you enter into last time with this copyright holder? How about terms and conditions in previous licenses with other copyright holders? Were those effective agreements, or did they cause problems? For instance, under your previous agreements, were you only able to make a single copy of an article from the CD-ROM for each library patron, or were you able to make class sets of 100?

KNOW WHAT YOU NEED

There is a difference between what you want and what you need. You may *want* a Porsche, but you *need* transportation of some sort. If someone offers you the Porsche at a price you can afford, then go for it. But if that just is not going to happen and someone gives you a good deal on a Hyundai, be reasonable.

When you license an online journal or database, you must first ask yourself how you will be using this particular content in your library. Are you aware of your patrons' needs, and how will you go about ensuring that those needs are met in your agreement? As set out in chapter 2, it is helpful, and perhaps essential, to put any legal agreement aside and to write a list of all the things that you and your patrons might do with the journal or database. For instance, will you need to negotiate rights to print out certain parts of it, or e-mail parts of it to yourself or to colleagues, or perhaps to copy it to a disk?

KNOW WHAT YOU WANT

Know what you can give up—for the right price. Always go to the negotiating table with a few items that you are willing to toss away altogether. They are called bargaining chips. They can be used to get something in return. Again, remember the difference between what you want and what you need. For instance, are you willing to be flexible with the delivery of the information, or is this unacceptable for what you plan on doing with the materials? If you toss out one of these want items in exchange for a break on a need item, then you are ahead of the game.

Be prepared for the possibility that you may not reach an agreement. Develop a set of alternatives for yourself. Is there someone else or another publisher you could approach for similar materials? How important are the materials to the library? You want to know your options and have an alternative plan should the negotiations come to a standstill or fail.

Write down your goals so you do not get lost in the moment of the negotiation. Know what you want and need.

KNOW YOUR PRICE

Know your price! How much are you willing to pay to license the materials? What is your library's budget for these particular materials? Is the budget flexible? If the publisher wants license fees based on the number of patrons, would the publisher be willing to accept a pay-per-use model? What are you willing to give up and at what price? Do not just toss items or clauses from the license to be agreeable. Negotiate those items you do not require for ones you do need.

WHO REPRESENTS THE LIBRARY?

Pick a person from your library to lead the negotiations. If your lawyer is negotiating the license, make sure this designated person from your library is also a part of all the negotiations. The librarian will likely need to educate the lawyer about librarianship and priorities and possibly lead the negotiation, using the lawyer more as a sounding board. It is important that a single person designated from your library participates in the negotiation process from the beginning to end. Changing your lead negotiator partway through the negotiations can lead to a waste of time and money, can be frustrating to both parties, and can lead to inconsistent negotiations. If you are negotiating as a team, make sure the team will proceed with the negotiation from beginning to end. Likewise, ask the content owner whether its representative will be the one negotiating the license, and insist that once this representative is selected, he or she will remain the negotiator throughout the process.

PLAN, PLAN . . . BUT BE FLEXIBLE

Plan your negotiations—decide when, where, who, and how. Setting the stage is important—even how the furniture is arranged can set the tone for the negotiations. For instance, one party sitting behind a big desk and the other party on the other side of it sets a much different tone from negotiating at a round table. Pick a place where you feel comfortable. If you feel better negotiating in your own office, choose this as the setting. If negotiations will take place in another setting, be sure to arrive fifteen minutes before your meeting. Get used to the surroundings. If you feel more comfortable with a mediator of some sort or an advisor, talk to the parties on the other side of the table and arrange for one. Note that negotiations need not take place in person, and may be done over the telephone or via e-mail.

TRY TO UNDERSTAND THE CONTENT OWNER

Know the party on the other side. This does not necessarily mean personally (although that too could be helpful). Know the corporation or content owner you are dealing with. Have some idea of their background, their financial situation, where their interests lie. Does the company want to expand into a certain market or create a reputation in a certain area? Can you be the door that the company uses to achieve those goals? If you are, then that may be one bargaining chip right there.

Be sure that you are negotiating with the appropriate party. Negotiating with someone who has no real power in the organization or who cannot make the decisions you are asking them to make is a waste of time. Find out who the decision makers are and talk to them. Make sure the party does indeed have ownership of the materials you want to license from them or that they have secured permissions from other copyright owners if necessary. If you are suspicious that the content owner may not in fact own the rights they are purporting to license to you, do not go any further. You should be comfortable that the content owner does in fact have legal authority to provide you with the rights set out in the license. A warranty clause in the license should reflect your comfort and not your suspicion.

During the Negotiations

LISTEN CAREFULLY AND ACTIVELY

Take in everything during the negotiations. The opposing party could provide you with valuable information that you can use to your advantage.

If you are unsure about something, ask for clarification so that there are no misunderstandings. Also, be sure that you understand exactly what it is you are hearing. Do not read something into what you are hearing and do not fill in gaps. Likewise, be careful not to miss anything that could turn out to be crucial.

ASK PROACTIVE QUESTIONS

Information librarians are well acquainted with the technique of asking proactive questions. "Yes" or "no" answers tell you very little. You need information and clues as to where the negotiations are heading. A librarian should feel right at home with this part of the process. License negotiations are very similar to the negotiations many librarians perform every day on the reference desk. The same skills used in the reference interview can be used in negotiating with a vendor. Just like in the reference interview, ask open-ended questions to get the other side to talk. Some individuals may be uncomfortable negotiating at all. If you are unable to get answers from the other party, perhaps changing the subject might be a good idea. For instance, if the other party is an artist, talking about the latest art exhibit might be a good way to get him to open up and then negotiations can proceed.

NEVER ASSUME ANYTHING

If you are unsure about what you just heard, ask them to repeat it. If something appears to be missing, ask them why. It bears repeating—do not fill in gaps or read items into a statement that are not there. For example, if the other party says he wants to monitor how his content is used, ask for clarification on how this is to be done and what sort of time and costs are involved. It is important to think in the long term about these issues. Being clear on these points will strengthen your license agreement by making it easier to ensure compliance to its terms once the content is in use.

BE ASSERTIVE—NOT AGGRESSIVE

You have a right to expect cooperation in negotiations. You have a right to ask for items on your "want" and "need" list. But you do not have a right to bully. Aggression is not negotiation. Aggression will rarely get you any-where—if anything, it may cause the other party to walk away from the table entirely, realizing that you as a customer or partner are more trouble than you are worth. Do not be too dogmatic about your position—you are there to negotiate.

COMMUNICATE CLEARLY AND NEUTRALLY

You are there as a representative of your library and do not have a personal stake in this negotiation. Neither does the party on the other side (usually). Do not compromise your own values and beliefs during the process. You are negotiating over a product, not a personality. Do not use double-talk or veiled allusions in an attempt to stymie the other party. If you do have a personal stake in it, you might want a more objective person to conduct the negotiations on your behalf.

TAKE NOTES

Taking notes is very important, particularly when the written agreement is presented for your approval. If something is missing or misrepresented, then it is far easier to refer to your notes and bring it and them to the attention of the other party. Also, frequently check the notes you made while preparing for the negotiations. Make sure you are on track with your goals and your needs. Date all of your notes so that they provide a chronology of your discussions. Keep in mind that any notes taken before, during, and after negotiations are not legally binding, and everything to which you agree should be clearly stated in the license.

BE ALERT

If the negotiation takes place in person, watch their, and your own, body language. If on the phone, listen for intonations, and if by fax or e-mail, look for any helpful signs in the language used to communicate.

CLEAR UP ANY MISUNDERSTANDINGS PROMPTLY

Negotiations commence and continue under an aura of trust. Part of that trust involves keeping the other party's goodwill. It is possible that innocent misunderstandings can destroy that aura of trust and finish your negotiations before they even get off the ground. Do not let misunderstandings get in the way of negotiations. Admitting that there was a misunderstanding is not a sign of weakness. Be honest. Do not bluff unless you definitely mean it. Bluffing does have its uses, but be prepared to carry through on the bluff if the other party calls it. If your negotiations include discussions of licensing terms and conditions with which you are unfamiliar, take time to consult a lawyer or colleagues.

KNOW WHEN TO TAKE A BREAK

Take some time during negotiations if things appear to be getting too heated. Take time if you have just been given a great deal of information to absorb. Take time if you need to consult with someone else. Ideas can come to you in the middle of negotiations for which you need approval before acting on them. The other party may toss out something on an unrelated matter that gives you some additional insight. Most importantly, *take some time to think over the deal before closing it.*

KNOW WHEN TO WALK AWAY

Lastly, know when to walk away—and do it. Do not be afraid to walk away from the negotiations if they are going nowhere. If you are not reaching your goals, then further negotiations are a waste of your time and theirs. Sometimes minds just cannot meet in the middle. Your time would be far better spent looking for another supplier of the same or similar content that may meet your needs. Now is the time to consider the alternatives to your negotiated agreement.

WHO SHOULD BE AT THE TABLE?

Librarians as the Drivers of Negotiation

For librarians, the license negotiation process is an opportunity to determine and define what uses of the licensed content will be permissible under what terms and conditions. Even if a lawyer is negotiating a license on your behalf, it is important for librarians to be involved in the negotiation process so the lawyer fully understands your needs and priorities. You do not want your lawyer to merely approach this as a legal challenge. You must keep in mind that you are the only voice or advocate for the rights of your patrons regarding their access to a particular information resource.

The Role of a Lawyer

In an ideal world (or at least in the ideal world of a lawyer!), every license agreement would be negotiated and drafted by and with the help of a lawyer. However, the reality in the library community is that librarians are often the ones who negotiate and even draft these agreements, and who must interpret them. Why? Because of the novelty of license agreements, there are few lawyers who are experts in this area, and in fact, there may be more librarians who are experienced with these agreements than lawyers. Often, the agreements are time-sensitive, and the library may not want to wait until its lawyer has had the opportunity to review the agreement, since the library wants to get immediate access to the content being licensed. Lawyers can be expensive, something not every library can afford. In addition, many institutions that do have in-house lawyers find that they can only provide general help and that the librarians must negotiate the specifics of the license. It is often best to use the lawyer as a sounding board and reviewer of the draft license, while the librarian does the negotiating. Thus, there is a great need for librarians to become more experienced in interpreting and negotiating licenses, as well as managing them.

Whether or not a lawyer is helping you with the negotiations, you should request that the agreement be in layperson's language. This will certainly ensure you understand what is being negotiated, but it will also help the librarians whose job it will be to interpret and apply the license.

NOTE

1. *Random House Unabridged Dictionary*, 2nd ed. (New York: Random House, 1993).

TIPS FOR NEGOTIATING

The following is a summary of the points set out in this chapter.

- Negotiation is not an "I win-you lose" affair.
- Negotiate both negotiable and nonnegotiable licenses.
- Never threaten the other party.
- Avoid oral agreements.
- Understand your patrons' needs.
- Be prepared by having all the information you need.
- Know what you can give up, and how much you can spend.
- If possible, one person from either side should be responsible for all negotiations.

(continued)

TIPS FOR NEGOTIATING—*continued*

- Write down your goals.
- Plan your negotiations.
- Know the party on the other side.
- Listen carefully and actively.
- Ask proactive questions.
- Never assume anything at any point. Always get clarification of even the smallest details.
- Be assertive—not aggressive.
- Communicate clearly and neutrally.
- Take notes, check them frequently, and use them often.
- Stay focused and on track with your needs.
- Watch body language.
- Clear up any misunderstandings promptly.
- Know when to take a break.
- Know when to walk away.

Questions and Answers
on Licensing

This chapter supplies answers to questions I have come across in the many seminars and workshops I have taught on digital licensing since 1997. In addition, in anticipation of this book on licensing, librarians from around the world e-mailed me questions they wanted addressed in this book. The questions below are designed to provide some specific answers to your questions, with the hope that the sharing of these questions and answers will help all librarians and content owners involved with digital licensing. In some ways, these questions may repeat various portions of this book, but laying them out in this easy-to-read format may help you learn more about digital licensing.

GENERAL LICENSING QUESTIONS

What would a "perfect" digital license contain?

There is no such thing as a perfect license. Each agreement must reflect the needs and requirements of the two parties involved. Although some model licenses have been developed, each situation is unique, and you must ensure that your license meets the particular needs of your library and the content owner with whom you are entering the license. The "perfect" digital license would be one that sets out terms and conditions which satisfy both the library and content owner.

Are a license and assignment the same thing?

No. A license is mere permission to use content according to specific terms and conditions. An assignment is an outright purchase of the rights to that content. Most content used by libraries is licensed.

Must all licenses be in writing?

They should be. This is not always necessary, but it is a good idea, since it is a good summary of your negotiations and constitutes a single document setting out the terms and conditions of use of content. It also helps in managing multiple digital licenses entered into by libraries. U.S. state law and Canadian provincial law have different requirements regarding when a legal agreement must be in writing.

What if the content owner does not provide you with a written license?

Ask about terms and conditions. Ask the content owner if there is a license with terms and conditions of use set out on his Web site or if he could e-mail or otherwise send you a copy of that license. If a license is not available, ask the content owner if he could set out the terms and conditions of use of the content in a letter to you so that you have a record of the nature of the license.

Does the term "digital licensing" imply that the licensed work is not in the public domain?

Yes. Generally, works that are licensed are protected by copyright. Works in the public domain are no longer protected by copyright; permission or a license is not necessary to use these works.

What if a license is not negotiable?

Most things are negotiable. Other than click-through, Webwrap, or shrinkwrap agreements, most licenses are subject to some discussion and negotiation. If you are faced with a license that does not meet your needs and does not appear to be negotiable, always ask the content owner about the portions of the license that you would like amended and try to open discussions and negotiations to ensure the final license meets your needs. See chapter 6 on negotiating licenses.

Why do some libraries get "deals" on their licenses?

A "deal" would mean that the library is satisfied with the terms and conditions it has negotiated in its license. In order to obtain the best possible license for your needs, know your library's needs, and learn to negotiate and communicate with the content owner. A deal may also be perceived as a special price, favorable terms and conditions, discounts based on existing relationships with the content owner, or a convenient length and scope of the license. Negotiating as a group or consortium may sometimes lead to special deals, as may a long-term relationship with a content owner.

Can you cross out parts of a license with which you do not agree?

Many license agreements are negotiable. Even if the agreement does not appear to be negotiable, you may still ask the other party if you may amend any particular clause or clauses. You may "cross out" portions of the license, but both parties should initial those crossed-out portions or any added penciled-in portions when they sign the agreement.

Our legal department will not approve the content owner's proposed license, but the content owner will not change the offending sections. What should we do?

This is a judgment call. Are you allowed to sign a license with which your legal department does not agree? Is it in your best interests to do so? Carefully examine the reason why your legal department is opposed to the license. Why is the content owner so inflexible about these offending sections? Will these sections be harmful to your library, or to the use of the licensed content? What is the liability of your library for including or omitting certain terms and conditions? Is it possible to obtain the same or similar content from another source? Perhaps the content is available through a consortium, which you could join, with terms your legal department could accept. Failing that, it would be worthwhile looking at your next best option: either finding another product that can at least come close to meeting your information needs, or finding the same one as part of a package with an aggregator, which would likely have different license terms.

Is our library responsible if one of our staff members, who does not have authority to do so, "signs" a click-through agreement to access online content?

It is possible that your library is legally liable for any such contracts. A prudent approach for any library is to ensure that its staff members are fully aware of the library's rights and obligations with regard to entering into online agreements. Also, it is helpful to inform staff members that they may bear responsibility when online agreements are entered into by a staff member who has no authority from the library to do so.

AIDS IN NEGOTIATING LICENSES

Are there model licenses that can be used in negotiating our library's license?

Yes. However, use these licenses with caution. There are several model licenses developed by various groups. However, caution should be taken when using these licenses, as they will undoubtedly need adaptation to fit your particular circumstances. It may be helpful to refer to more than one of these licenses to benefit from the accumulated knowledge put into creating these models. Chapter 2 discusses various examples of model licenses.

How can licensing principles endorsed by a library association help our library in negotiating our licenses?

You may use them as a checklist. Similar to model licenses, licensing principles can be a helpful guiding source in developing your own library's licensing policy and in negotiating licenses. However, use these principles with caution and as a checklist, as opposed to following them blindly, and adapt them to meet your particular needs and circumstances.

Is it necessary for our library to have a licensing policy before entering into negotiations?

No. A library licensing policy is not part of the negotiations with content owners and in fact should be kept confidential to your library. The purpose of this policy is to act as an internal guide in setting out a consistent approach for negotiating all licenses. It should be based on a consensus of information from various people and past experiences to help guide you through the negotiation process, setting out goals and bottom lines for your library. In many ways, a licensing policy is developed through the same means as your library's acquisitions policy. Licensing policies are discussed in chapter 2.

CONTENT-SPECIFIC ISSUES

Are all databases protected by copyright?

No. The current U.S. copyright law requires that a collection of materials or a database involve some creativity in order to obtain copyright protection. Thus, mere skill and labor in compiling a database is not sufficient to acquire copyright protection. Note that in Canada, a database may be protected if compiled with skill, labor, and judgment. At the time of writing this book, there is ongoing debate in the United States as to what sort of legislation should protect databases that are not protected by copyright law.

Are digital images scanned from nondigital images protected by copyright?

Neither U.S. nor Canadian copyright law is clear on this issue. However, it seems that a "mere" scanning or digitization of an image would not result in a new copyright work. If there is a certain level of skill, effort, and talent involved in the creation of a digital work, then it is possible that there is copyright in the new digital work. Even if there is no copyright in the digital version, one may license the "access" to the digital work.

Are maps protected by licenses?

Check what your license says about including maps. The subject matter protected by your license depends on what you have agreed upon. The license may extend to a database, or to periodical articles. It might include an encyclopedia, or it may refer to maps and charts. You must look at your specific license to see what is covered by it. If you need to use specific content that is not covered by your license, negotiate for the inclusion of that content in your license.

May my library reproduce a photograph that does not have any copyright information stamped on it?

No. The fact that a photograph or other work lacks copyright information does not mean that you may automatically use it. You must seek permission from the owner of that photograph. You may have to be creative to locate the copyright owner or to use a different photograph in which you can clear copyright permission. Note that in Canada, you may apply for an unlocatable copyright owner license from the Copyright Board in cases where you cannot locate the copyright owner. See also http://www.cb-cda.gc.ca/indexe.html.

BEFORE THE NEGOTIATIONS BEGIN

How does a library determine what rights need to be in the license?

Determine what uses of the content will be made, and then ensure that the license reflects these uses. It is best to determine these rights independently of reviewing the license offered to you, in order to ensure that you are meeting your needs and not merely reacting to the offer from the content

owner. Consult various people in your library, from the lawyer to the acquisitions librarian to the reference librarian. You should even consult your
patrons where possible.

Is it possible to sample some of the content before we sign the license?

This is something you would want to discuss with the content owner. As the
popularity of digital content is still growing, it is possible that your patrons
may not find certain content helpful in a digital form. In specific circumstances, you may want to "test" this out with them by gaining "test access" to
that content before signing a license. You may also wish to test the format of
the content to ensure it is compatible with your intended uses.

*Does the publisher/distributor/aggregator always own the content
being licensed?*

In some situations, you will license content directly from the owner of the
content. However, in many situations, you will be licensing from a publisher, distributor, or aggregator who has rights to license content owned by
someone else. In either situation, you should feel comfortable that the licensor does actually have the rights to license the content to you. If you are
doubtful of this, look for a different licensor. Also, it is always prudent to
include a warranty clause in the license that states something to the effect
that the licensor does actually have the rights to license that content to you.
(However, do not rely on this—make sure they are trustworthy!)

What does "third-party rights" mean?

It means that the content is owned by a third party, or someone other than
the publisher, distributor, or aggregator who is licensing the content to you.
In this situation, you want to ensure that the publisher, distributor, or aggregator has the rights from the content owner to license that content.

DEFINING WORDS IN LICENSES

How do we know what words mean in our existing licenses?

Check your licenses for a definitions section which defines terminology for
the purposes of that particular license. Sometimes there is no specific
section for definitions, and words are instead defined throughout the license
when they first appear.

*Where can we find definitions of words that we need to include
in the definition section of our license?*

There are some technology dictionaries that might be helpful, but because
you want to define the words for the specific purposes of your license, it is
best to ask library staff, including any technology-related persons, how to
define the terms for your purposes. Sometimes the definitions will have to
be negotiated with the content owner, since different meanings given to different words can affect the terms and conditions of the license.

Is there a definition of "commercial use"?

There is no single definition of the term "commercial use." It is up to the
content owner and the library to define "commercial use" in a manner that
meets the needs of the license. This may be negotiable.

*Does "personal use" in a license include an individual researcher
who is paid $30 an hour for his or her research?*

There is no set definition of "personal use." For each license, "personal use"
should be defined to meet the needs of that particular license and arrangement.

FAIR USE AND INTERLIBRARY LOAN

*Is fair use/fair dealing applicable when content is subject
to a license agreement?*

If the agreement does not mention fair use/fair dealing, then fair use/fair
dealing is still applicable. However, the license may limit the scope of fair
use/fair dealing. This is something you may wish to discuss with the content
owner. See chapters 3 and 4 for more information.

*Our publisher has included in our license exclusions to fair use, which
they have always allowed for print documents. What should we do?*

If you would like fair use to apply to the licensed content, then you must let
the publisher know this. Ask them why they are excluding fair use, and try
to come to a middle ground on how you may include fair use in a manner
with which the publisher is comfortable.

May a license prohibit interlibrary loans?

Yes. A license may prohibit interlibrary loans. However, this may be a point
of negotiation.

*Why does the same publisher allow interlibrary loans for a print
copy of a journal, but not for an electronic copy?*

Many publishers are concerned that electronic copies of content will be distributed further than their intended audience. For instance, if one library electronically lends a journal to another library, the publisher may have little control over who else may access the electronic copy. Unlike distributing print journals, an electronic journal can instantaneously be e-mailed to hundreds and thousands of people around the world in seconds. In some situations, publishers will allow a print copy of an electronic article to be loaned to another library, but the same article in an electronic form may not be loaned. This is something you will need to address in your license.

AUTHORIZED SITES

*Can a library patron in Australia legally access content from
our U.S.-based library?*

If your library is providing access to patrons outside your own country, or if patrons from your library may access the content while outside the country, you will need to address this in your license and ensure that the authorized users and authorized site clauses allow for this.

*We are a countywide system with ten locations spread throughout
a very large county. However, we provide service to our libraries through
one location. Would a license agreement cover our entire system?*

Your license agreements should reflect the fact that your service is provided through one library, but that users of the digital content may be from any of the ten libraries in the county. This should be an explicit clause or be defined in the license. You want to make sure that the content owner knows and agrees with the ways in which the content is used by your patrons.

AUTHORIZED USERS

*If I negotiate a license for thirty professionals in our company, will
their support staff and researchers also have access to that content?*

No. It is very important that all authorized users are specified in your license. Before signing the license, ensure that you know who will be accessing the licensed content and try to define them in the license.

*Are "walk-in users" able to have access to content licensed
for our educational institution?*

Only if they are defined as "authorized users" in the license. If your library has a number of "walk-in users" who will want to access the digital content, then you should negotiate for their specific inclusion in the license.

In an academic library, are alumni allowed access under a license?

This is something that you would have to negotiate. Alumni may be covered by a clause allowing the general public to access the licensed content. However, if specific users such as faculty, students, etc., are set out as authorized users, then you will have to specifically include alumni as authorized users.

*How do you ensure that a licensee includes the licensor's copyright
notice when a licensee accesses the licensed content?*

This may be included in the license agreement. It is not uncommon to see a clause that states something to the effect that a copyright notice in the name of the licensor must be included whenever the content is used, i.e., displayed, published, reproduced, etc.

*We have content we licensed directly from copyright holders that
we are now sublicensing to an online database publisher. Do we need
to obtain any additional permissions to sublicense the content?*

Unless your initial license with the content holders included the right to sublicense that content to a third party such as an online database publisher, you will require additional rights to do this.

RECORD-KEEPING

May publishers require record-keeping of the use of licensed content?

Publishers may request record-keeping of who is accessing the licensed content, when, for how long, and what amount or portion of the content is being accessed. However, a library should be very cautious in agreeing to record-keeping in any detail. This is in part due to the invasion of privacy, and also in part because of the expense and time involved in such record-keeping. If the content owner is asking for unreasonable record-keeping, try to negotiate less onerous record-keeping.

Why do publishers need record-keeping of the use of licensed content?

Publishers frequently have to report on the use of the licensed content to the original content holder. Be creative in discussing and working with publishers to find procedures used to track and report on licensed uses. There are many ways in which procedures can meet the library's need for confidentiality, as well as meeting the publisher's need for accountability. Your library and the publisher need to come to a satisfactory arrangement for reporting licensed uses.

How do we protect the names of our users or patrons?

Your library may want to include a clause in the license that states something to the effect that it will not disclose specific names of users of the licensed content.

FREQUENTLY NEGOTIATED AREAS

How can our library avoid entering into the same license year after year?

You can negotiate a license for a longer duration of time than one year. Alternatively, you may negotiate a clause for automatic renewal upon certain circumstances so that if the license is working well, you do not need to renegotiate it each year.

*What if the content owner wants a higher fee for the content
than my library can afford?*

If you cannot negotiate a lower fee for the electronic content, try the strategy of narrowing the terms and conditions of use for that lower fee you are offering. For instance, try to restrict the number of users that will have access to the content. Reduce the number of years to be covered in the license.

If a license does not mention "electronic archiving," would this be allowed?

It depends on the wording of the grant of rights clause. You must carefully review the grant of rights to see whether electronic archiving is either specifically or implicitly included. If implicitly included, you may want to specifically include mention of this use of the content.

*If a licensee wishes to reproduce or republish in print form content
for which only a digital license has been obtained, is this permissible
under the digital license?*

Generally, a digital license will only provide permission for digital uses of the specified content. Unless the license also permits print uses, you may need to include a clause relating to print uses.

WARRANTIES AND INDEMNITIES

Can your warranty and indemnity protect you from a content holder who does not really hold the rights to the content being licensed?

It is always best to enter into any licenses or negotiations with content owners whom you trust. If you are suspicious that the content owner does not own some or all of the rights being licensed, it is best to terminate your negotiations and to find and work with a more trustworthy content owner. Although a warranty and indemnity may protect you to some degree, they can be expensive to enforce, and the content owner may not in fact have the funds to indemnify you against any losses or legal fees resulting from using content that belongs to another party.

ISSUES AFTER SIGNING THE LICENSE

What if the content is not available throughout the duration of the license?

This is something you should consider before signing the license. Ask the content owner for some guarantee as to the length of downtime for maintenance, etc., and for either a reduction in the license fee or an extension in the license to compensate for downtime beyond this amount. You should consider a clause in your license to get out of the contract obligations or at least obtain a reduction of license fees should the content not be available throughout the duration of the license.

What if our library needs a right that is not included in the license, for instance, the right of a patron to e-mail herself a copy of an article from a licensed database?

If the right is not specifically included in the license, or cannot be interpreted as an authorized use in other rights granted or permitted uses, then the patron is unable to e-mail the article to herself. If necessary, you may be able to amend the license with the content owner, or to include this right when the licensed is renewed.

How does a library know if its license will automatically renew?

This is something that would have to be addressed in the license. If the license does not deal with automatic renewal, then the license will not automatically renew at the time of expiration. If you would like automatic renewal, negotiate this in your license.

Does the content owner or the library have the onus to renew the license?

Either party may approach the other about renewing the license. It is a good idea for a library to keep a database of licenses and their renewal dates. This way, you can ensure you have ongoing access to licensed content and that agreements are renewed prior to their expiration date.

Can our library archive licensed content and provide access to it after the license has expired?

That would depend on what your license states. If this is not addressed in your license, then you should not be making archive copies or providing access to these copies after the expiration of the license. Having access to previously licensed content is an issue that is controversial and is difficult to address in a license. It is the subject of much discussion among libraries and publishers, and these discussions are well worth following.

YOUR QUESTIONS AND ANSWERS

As you proceed through various negotiations, you will find that the same questions unique to your situation arise again and again. It may be helpful to keep a list of these questions and answers and include them in your licensing policy. Do not forget to update the list on a regular basis.

Go License!

A verbal contract isn't worth the paper it is written on.
—Sam Goldwyn, Hollywood film producer

Now that you understand the concepts of licensing and the various clauses you may include in your license, you may be wondering what is the appropriate type of licensing arrangement for you.

When licensing content, you will have to decide vis-à-vis each license, based on the particular circumstances, what is the appropriate type of arrangement and how you should set this out in your agreement. At one extreme is a simple one-page document identifying the parties, the content being used, the purpose of the use, length of use, payment, the rights being licensed, with a warranty that the content is in fact owned by the party who is licensing it, and bearing the signatures of both parties. At the other extreme may be a twenty-page agreement full of legal terminology.

Put your effort into negotiating when it is most needed. When you are thinking about the time and energy you will give to each license, look at the cost-benefits of doing so. Can you use a simple one-page license for a short time frame or to license a smaller piece of content? Or does the use of the licensed content require full-scale negotiations of all clauses and drafting of an extensive license covering multiple years? Examine standard licenses offered to you by publishers; in some situations, they may be the answer to a quicker negotiation process. Do not assume that you need to negotiate each clause in every license; see what works for you, then discuss any specific needs with the content owner that would better meet the needs of your library.

Lengthier agreements make the negotiating and signing process more time-consuming and costly, and are more difficult to complete. In addition, a twenty-page contract landing on your desk is fairly intimidating, and given the opportunity to license an alternative electronic product with a simple license, you would seize that chance.

PLAIN LANGUAGE

Wherever possible, it is important to urge content owners to offer licenses written in plain, nonlegal language and to be "library friendly." One example of plain language is to avoid terms like "Licensor" and "Licensee" and instead to simply use "Jane Content Owner" and "the Library."

It is important, however, that key issues are addressed in the agreement and that brevity does not mean an omission of important clauses. One way to keep an agreement short is to set out the agreement as simply as possible, without specific details, in a "main" agreement, and then to append details such as license fees or a payment schedule as separate attachments to the main agreement. This approach is advantageous to content owners because they may then have one standard license agreement, with any changes or additions for each specific license dealt with in an appendix. This would lessen the administrative burden for publishers who over time may have different license agreements with different libraries. Libraries may find this helpful for similar reasons.

A WRITTEN LICENSE

Get it in writing. Never base your licensing arrangements on assumptions or conversations.

The importance of having a written agreement cannot be stressed enough. Although it is not legally mandatory in all situations, it will provide you with a summary of your agreement concerning how you may use the electronic content. It will also be of great benefit when an issue arises over the conditions of licensing the content and you have a written document to consult. Also, personnel change all the time; if a content owner and a library negotiate a license, and the negotiator for either party moves on to a different position, the terms and conditions of the license may be lost if they are not reduced to writing.

CHANGING CLAUSES

When you negotiate various changes to a license agreement, sometimes it is necessary to correct these changes on your word processor and to work with a clean copy of the license. When doing this, make sure both parties are aware that changes have been made to the license. In other circumstances, where the changes are minor, you may strike and handwrite the negotiated changes, then each party should initial each change or each page of the license when they sign it.

YOUR PARTICULAR CIRCUMSTANCES

Throughout this book, you have been reminded that each license may be unique for each type of licensed content. Thus, you must always keep in mind your particular circumstances in negotiating a license. View every licensed content with a fresh eye with respect to the appropriate terms and conditions for that particular content.

Notwithstanding the need to meet your particular circumstances, you will want to balance in the fact that it would be easiest for your library to use consistent terms and conditions in each license, and have similar definitions of, for example, "authorized uses" and "authorized users." This would make license compliance much easier further down the road. It may also make interface design easier in those cases where your library has a Web page and is providing access to the licensed content from its page or through campus machines or a proxy server. It will be much more difficult if you are forced to divide up the patrons at the library into different classes of users and have to run more than one proxy server, one for each group, in order for your library to provide access remotely and still comply with your licenses.

MANAGING MULTIPLE LICENSES

Although your library may have only a handful of signed digital licenses at the current time, it is never too early to initiate a system to manage them. The number of licenses your library has signed may increase rapidly over a short period of time, and it may become increasingly difficult to quickly determine which terms of use apply to which licensed content.

You might consider creating a simple database setting out the content owner's name, e-mail address and telephone number, the licensed content, what uses are permitted, who are the authorized users, from what sites may the content be accessed, when the license expires, and whether it is automatically renewable. Of course, there are many more items you may include in the database, and the checklists in chapters 4 and 5 provide valuable headings for any such database. Software for a standard database may meet your needs for managing your licenses, though you may prefer customized computer software to help you do so.

CHANGING TECHNOLOGY AND NEEDS

It is possible and even likely that the license agreement you enter into today will not be as effective tomorrow. Although a license agreement may meet all of your current technological needs when signed, within a short time your technological needs may change and you may require different or new uses of the licensed content, or a modification of certain terms and conditions in order to be able to effectively use the licensed content. Modifications may need to be made to the agreement for economic, technological, legal, or other reasons.

Some ways to address rapidly and constantly changing technology have been discussed throughout this book. These suggestions include:

Short-term license agreement

Short-term agreement with automatic renewals (unless notification by one party)

Amendment clause (see chapter 5 to allow for any changes in the agreement)

Trial license period to enable both the content owner and library to work out problems, discover and solve specific issues, or seek out technological solutions

Library/customer support which allows libraries to understand the license agreement from the perspective of the content owner. To go further, support could report to the content owner or library any issues or problems that require discussion or inclusion in subsequent license agreements. Feedback forms could be placed on the library's site for this purpose.

Reduction of license fee in certain circumstances. For example, should the content owner have to remove some of the licensed content specified in the license, then the library should be entitled to a refund on a pro rata basis of its license fee. Also, should the licensed content not be available for a lengthy period of time, the library may be entitled to some reduction or refund of the license fee.

FRUSTRATION AND PATIENCE

Along with license agreements often comes frustration. There is frustration in the fact that libraries now have to enter into legal agreements just to access content for their "shelves." There is frustration that access to lawyers is not always available or immediate, and that it can be costly. There is frustration that technology outdates agreements that seem perfectly fine at the time of signing them. There is frustration that electronic uses of content must be monitored or regulated to some degree, whereas patrons can freely roam libraries' print bookshelves without the same restrictions. There is frustration that the party with whom you are negotiating a license knows less than you, and actually makes the negotiating process more difficult. Further, there is the cost and time in negotiating a license which does not exist when acquiring print materials.

Unfortunately, there is no magic answer to overcoming these and other frustrations. Yes, time will probably ease some frustrations (though it could possibly raise others!). It is best to enter into any license negotiations with an open mind, lots of patience, and hopefully at the end of the day, you will acquire the content and license that best meet your needs.

FURTHER THOUGHTS

Licensing has become a part of life and day-to-day duties for librarians. The knowledge and skills of librarians in this area are growing rapidly. Knowing your library's goals, understanding clauses that appear in licenses, and entering into the negotiation process with a flexible view and authority from your library will result in licenses that meet your needs. Effective communication throughout the process with those in your own library as well as with the content owner will ensure a smoother and more effective process.

Licensing content for digital media is new to everyone. While trends are beginning to emerge, digital licensing is still in its infancy. Although the lack of standardization can be frustrating, it also allows for creativity and experimentation, as well as time to reflect upon the needs of content owners and libraries. Consideration of the issues and clauses discussed in this book and ongoing discussions with content owners, librarians, and lawyers negotiating licenses will help develop a coherent, consistent approach in your licensing.

There is no one *right* way. The best agreement is the one that meets your library's needs and builds a strong relationship with the content owner. Both sides are aiming at fair access at a fair fee.

In any licensing situation, you must examine your own perspectives and goals, as well as those of the other party. It is important to tailor your negotiations and agreements to match your particular circumstances. Keep in mind that there is room for creativity in your licenses.

As with all agreements, it is best, where feasible, to consult a lawyer before signing on the dotted line, as opposed to consulting one at a later stage when a dispute arises. A well-written license agreement will clearly set out the relationship between the parties and the details of the content being licensed. In many cases, a good license agreement may help you avoid disputes in the future. It will be a document you refer to again and again when questions arise during the course of your relationship, either as a licensor or licensee—and hopefully, it will provide you with answers.

Section 107 of the U.S. Copyright Act on Fair Use

§ 107. Limitations on exclusive rights: Fair use

Notwithstanding the provisions of sections 106 and 106A, the fair use of a copyrighted work, including such use by reproduction in copies or phonorecords or by any other means specified by that section, for purposes such as criticism, comment, news reporting, teaching (including multiple copies for classroom use), scholarship, or research, is not an infringement of copyright. In determining whether the use made of a work in any particular case is a fair use the factors to be considered shall include—

(1) the purpose and character of the use, including whether such use is of a commercial nature or is for nonprofit educational purposes;

(2) the nature of the copyrighted work;

(3) the amount and substantiality of the portion used in relation to the copyrighted work as a whole; and

(4) the effect of the use upon the potential market for or value of the copyrighted work.

The fact that a work is unpublished shall not itself bar a finding of fair use if such finding is made upon consideration of all the above factors.

Section 108 of the U.S. Copyright Act on Interlibrary Loan

§ 108. Limitations on exclusive rights: Reproduction by libraries and archives

(a) Except as otherwise provided in this title and notwithstanding the provisions of section 106, it is not an infringement of copyright for a library or archives, or any of its employees acting within the scope of their employment, to reproduce no more than one copy or phonorecord of a work, except as provided in subsections (b) and (c), or to distribute such copy or phonorecord, under the conditions specified by this section, if—

   (1) the reproduction or distribution is made without any purpose of direct or indirect commercial advantage;

   (2) the collections of the library or archives are
      (i) open to the public, or
      (ii) available not only to researchers affiliated with the library or archives or with the institution of which it is a part, but also to other persons doing research in a specialized field; and

   (3) the reproduction or distribution of the work includes a notice of copyright that appears on the copy or phonorecord that is reproduced under the provisions of this section, or includes a legend stating that the work may be protected by copyright if no such notice can be found on the copy or phonorecord that is reproduced under the provisions of this section.

(b) The rights of reproduction and distribution under this section apply to three copies or phonorecords of an unpublished work duplicated solely for purposes of preservation and security or for deposit for research use in another library or archives of the type described by clause (2) of subsection (a), if—

   (1) the copy or phonorecord reproduced is currently in the collections of the library or archives; and

   (2) any such copy or phonorecord that is reproduced in digital format is not otherwise distributed in that format and is not made available to the public in that format outside the premises of the library or archives.

(c) The right of reproduction under this section applies to three copies or phonorecords of a published work duplicated solely for the purpose of replacement of a copy or phonorecord that is damaged, deteriorating, lost, or stolen, or if the existing format in which the work is stored has become obsolete, if—

(1) the library or archives has, after a reasonable effort, determined that an unused replacement cannot be obtained at a fair price; and

(2) any such copy or phonorecord that is reproduced in digital format is not made available to the public in that format outside the premises of the library or archives in lawful possession of such copy.

For purposes of this subsection, a format shall be considered obsolete if the machine or device necessary to render perceptible a work stored in that format is no longer manufactured or is no longer reasonably available in the commercial marketplace.

(d) The rights of reproduction and distribution under this section apply to a copy, made from the collection of a library or archives where the user makes his or her request or from that of another library or archives, of no more than one article or other contribution to a copyrighted collection or periodical issue, or to a copy or phonorecord of a small part of any other copyrighted work, if—

(1) the copy or phonorecord becomes the property of the user, and the library or archives has had no notice that the copy or phonorecord would be used for any purpose other than private study, scholarship, or research; and

(2) the library or archives displays prominently, at the place where orders are accepted, and includes on its order form, a warning of copyright in accordance with requirements that the Register of Copyrights shall prescribe by regulation.

(e) The rights of reproduction and distribution under this section apply to the entire work, or to a substantial part of it, made from the collection of a library or archives where the user makes his or her request or from that of another library or archives, if the library or archives has first determined, on the basis of a reasonable investigation, that a copy or phonorecord of the copyrighted work cannot be obtained at a fair price, if—

(1) the copy or phonorecord becomes the property of the user, and the library or archives has had no notice that the copy or phonorecord would be used for any purpose other than private study, scholarship, or research; and

(2) the library or archives displays prominently, at the place where orders are accepted, and includes on its order form, a warning of copyright in accordance with requirements that the Register of Copyrights shall prescribe by regulation.

(f) Nothing in this section—

(1) shall be construed to impose liability for copyright infringement upon a library or archives or its employees for the unsupervised use of reproducing

equipment located on its premises: *Provided,* That such equipment displays a notice that the making of a copy may be subject to the copyright law;

(2) excuses a person who uses such reproducing equipment or who requests a copy or phonorecord under subsection (d) from liability for copyright infringement for any such act, or for any later use of such copy or phonorecord, if it exceeds fair use as provided by section 107;

(3) shall be construed to limit the reproduction and distribution by lending of a limited number of copies and excerpts by a library or archives of an audio-visual news program, subject to clauses (1), (2), and (3) of subsection (a); or

(4) in any way affects the right of fair use as provided by section 107, or any contractual obligations assumed at any time by the library or archives when it obtained a copy or phonorecord of a work in its collections.

(g) The rights of reproduction and distribution under this section extend to the isolated and unrelated reproduction or distribution of a single copy or phonorecord of the same material on separate occasions, but do not extend to cases where the library or archives, or its employee-

(1) is aware or has substantial reason to believe that it is engaging in the related or concerted reproduction or distribution of multiple copies or phonorecords of the same material, whether made on one occasion or over a period of time, and whether intended for aggregate use by one or more individuals or for separate use by the individual members of a group; or

(2) engages in the systematic reproduction or distribution of single or multiple copies or phonorecords of material described in subsection (d): *Provided,* That nothing in this clause prevents a library or archives from participating in interlibrary arrangements that do not have, as their purpose or effect, that the library or archives receiving such copies or phonorecords for distribution does so in such aggregate quantities as to substitute for a subscription to or purchase of such work.

(h) (1) For purposes of this section, during the last 20 years of any term of copyright of a published work, a library or archives, including a nonprofit educational institution that functions as such, may reproduce, distribute, display, or perform in facsimile or digital form a copy or phonorecord of such work, or portions thereof, for purposes of preservation, scholarship, or research, if such library or archives has first determined, on the basis of a reasonable investigation, that none of the conditions set forth in subparagraphs (A), (B), and (C) of paragraph (2) apply.

(2) No reproduction, distribution, display, or performance is authorized under this subsection if—

(A) the work is subject to normal commercial exploitation;

(B) a copy or phonorecord of the work can be obtained at a reasonable price; or

(C) the copyright owner or its agent provides notice pursuant to regulations promulgated by the Register of Copyrights that either of the conditions set forth in subparagraphs (A) and (B) applies.

(3) The exemption provided in this subsection does not apply to any subsequent uses by users other than such library or archives.

(i) The rights of reproduction and distribution under this section do not apply to a musical work, a pictorial, graphic or sculptural work, or a motion picture or other audiovisual work other than an audiovisual work dealing with news, except that no such limitation shall apply with respect to rights granted by subsections (b) and (c), or with respect to pictorial or graphic works published as illustrations, diagrams, or similar adjuncts to works of which copies are reproduced or distributed in accordance with subsections (d) and (e).

GLOSSARY

The following are definitions of words and phrases commonly found in licensing agreements.

acceptance   the formal act of agreeing to an offer to enter into a legally binding agreement.

access   the ability to gain entry to a database or other digital information.

agreement   an understanding between two or more parties that is often embodied in a legally binding, written contract.

amendment   an addition to the terms of an agreement. *See also* modification.

archive copy   a copy of a work intended to be preserved permanently.

assignment   a transfer of all or part of the contractual rights and/or obligations to another party.

authentication   a process by which the identity of a user accessing a network or other source of information is verified.

authorized signature   the signature of a person with authority and power to represent and legally bind a party to a written agreement.

authorized use, permitted use   use of information that is expressly allowed under a licensing agreement.

authorized user, permitted user   a person designated in a licensing agreement as having permission to access or otherwise use the digital information that is the subject matter of the agreement.

backup copy   a temporary copy of digital information made for recovery purposes.

breach   a breaking of a promise or a failure to perform an obligation under an agreement.

click-on license, click-through license   *see* shrinkwrap agreement.

---

concurrent use   the simultaneous use of digital information by more than one user; often used as a measure of limitations on the use of digital information.

confidentiality   the treating of information as private and not for distribution beyond specifically identified individuals or organizations, nor used other than for specifically identified purposes.

contract   a formal, legally binding agreement between two or more parties.

copies   reproductions of all or a portion of digital information onto any one of a number of media, including computer diskette, hard-copy printout, or by exact quotation.

copyright   legally granted property rights in intellectual works embodied in some physical means of expression, such as print, musical score, or electronic image.

coursepacks   copies of materials assembled by instructors to be used by students in a class, usually in lieu of or in addition to a textbook.

dial-up access   access to digital materials through connection with a remote server through a modem or other remote access device.

disclaimer   a statement denying responsibility for a particular action.

display   information that appears on the screen of a computer terminal.

distributor   an individual or organization that resells, sublicenses, or otherwise makes digital information available from the owner to end-users.

domain   a group of computers linked to the Internet whose host names share a common suffix, such as ".com" (commercial), ".edu" (educational), or ".net" (communications network).

download   to copy digital information onto a hard drive, diskette, or other electronic storage medium.

end-user   an individual or organization that accesses digital information for their own use.

fair use   the right set forth in Section 107 of the United States Copyright Act to use copyrighted materials for certain purposes, such as criticism, comment, news reporting, teaching, scholarship, and research. Section 107 sets out four factors to be considered in determining whether or not a particular use is fair: (1) the purpose and character of the use, including whether such use is of a commercial nature or is for nonprofit educational purposes; (2) the nature of the copyrighted work; (3) the amount and substantiality of the portion used in relation to the copyrighted work as a whole; and (4) the effect of the use upon the potential market for or value of the copyrighted work.

force majeure   literally, "greater force"; a clause designed to protect against failures to perform contractual obligations caused by unavoidable events beyond the party's control, such as natural disasters or wars.

governing law   the jurisdiction whose law will be applied in the event of a dispute relating to an agreement.

host name   a unique name used to identify a computer on a network.

indemnity   one party's agreement to insure or otherwise defend another party against any claims by third parties resulting from performance under the agreement.

infringement   an unauthorized use of material protected by copyright, patent, or trademark law.

interlibrary loan (ILL)   the loan of materials owned or licensed by one library to another library or its users.

Internet   a worldwide system of interconnected networks and computers.

Internet Protocol (IP)   a standard developed to identify computers and networks linked to the Internet.

IP address   a unique identifier of computers or networks linked to the Internet.

liability   legal responsibility for an act or failure to act.

license   permission to do something which, without such permission, would be illegal. For example, a license to use digital information gives the licensee permission to access and use the information under the terms and conditions described in the agreement between the licensor and the licensee.

license agreement   a written contract setting forth the terms under which a licensor grants a license to a licensee.

licensee   the person or entity that is given permission through a license to access or otherwise use digital information. The licensee, often a library or an educational or research organization, generally pays the licensor a fee for permission to use digital information.

licensor   the person or entity that gives or grants a license. The licensor owns or has permission to distribute digital materials to a licensee.

local area network (LAN)   a network linking two or more computers and peripheral devices in a specific geographic area.

modification   a change or alteration to the terms of an agreement. *See also* amendment.

negotiations   communications between two or more parties towards the development and maintenance of contractual relationships.

network   a group of computers linked together to share information. Networks can consist of a number of linked computers in a specific physical location, a local area network (LAN), or they may consist of computers located at different physical sites linked together by means of phone lines and modems or other forms of long-distance communications.

node a specific connection point in a network.

nonassignable a licensing agreement or the rights, obligations, and terms thereof that may not be assigned to any party who is not a signatory to the agreement. For example, a library licensee may not assign the right to access licensed materials to another library. *See also* nontransferable.

nondisclosure an agreement to treat specific information confidentially. *See also* confidentiality.

nonexclusive rights granted to a licensee under a licensing agreement that are not given only to that licensee; the licensor reserves the right to give the same or similar rights to use the licensed materials to other parties.

nontransferable a licensing agreement or the rights, obligations, and terms thereof that may not be sold, given, assigned, or otherwise conveyed to any party who is not a signatory to the agreement. For example, a library licensee may not sell or give the right to access licensed materials to another library. *See also* nonassignable.

penalty a specific cost to be assessed against a party for breach of a term of an agreement.

permitted use *see* authorized use.

permitted user *see* authorized user.

perpetual license the continuing right to access digital information after the termination of a license agreement.

public access terminals terminals that are made available to the patrons of a library or other research institution for use by the general public.

remedies the special rights a party has when another party defaults or breaches an agreement. Remedies include lawsuits or injunctions to stop an action that may harm a party.

remote access the ability to access and use digital information from a location off-site from where the information is physically located.

rights powers or privileges granted by an agreement or law.

security means used to protect against the unauthorized use of and to prevent unauthorized access to digital information.

server a computer that stores digital information to be "served" to other computers or workstations through a network or by dial-up access.

severability a clause which provides that in the event that one or more provisions of an agreement are declared void or unenforceable, the balance of the agreement remains in force. Such provisions may also be referred to as "separability clauses."

shrinkwrap agreement the method by which electronic information providers establish the terms under which users may gain access to the information without any negotiation with the user. The term developed in connection with the purchase of software. Ordinarily, software is provided in a box enclosed in a plastic wrap known as "shrinkwrap." The box would state that by removing the shrinkwrap from it, the purchaser of the software was agreeing to the terms of a licensing agreement included inside the box. The term "shrinkwrap agreement" has been expanded to include the presentation of licensing agreements to software buyers and information users before the program will permit use of the product or information. Known also as "click-on" or "click-through" licenses, this process requires users to affirmatively click on a button indicating their acceptance of the licensing agreement before they can install the software or view the information.

　　While the issue of shrinkwraps is not settled in all jurisdictions, the trend in the law has been to consider such agreements enforceable and binding, provided that the user has the opportunity to return the product for a full refund in the event that he or she does not wish to be bound by the terms of the agreement.

site as used in a licensing agreement, a "site" is a physical location affiliated with the licensee where the licensee may permit access to digital information to authorized users.

site license a particular type of licensing agreement that permits the access and use of digital information at a specific site.

subscription a type of licensing agreement by which a licensee pays for access to digital information by means of a periodic fee.

term 1: a word or phrase; an expression, particularly one that has been defined in an agreement; 2: a clause or provision of an agreement; 3: a fixed and definite period of time. The term of a licensing agreement is the period of time during which the agreement is in effect.

terminal a computer workstation, linked to a server or other computer over a network, on which a user may display information. When it is merely a video display, it may be referred to as a "dumb terminal."

termination the cancellation or ending of an agreement.

third party a party who is not a signatory to an agreement but who may nevertheless have rights and obligations relating to that agreement.

unauthorized user a person designated in a licensing agreement as not having permission to access or otherwise use the digital information that is the subject matter of the agreement or, more often, any person who is not an authorized user, as that term is defined.

venue the particular jurisdiction where a legal dispute is tried.

waiver the intentional or voluntary relinquishment of a known right or privilege granted under an agreement, or the failure to take advantage of some failure of performance or other wrong. For example, if a licensee fails to complain about a series of interruptions in connecting to a licensor's database, the licensor may later claim that the licensee has waived any claim that the service interruptions constituted a breach of the license agreement.

warranty a statement or representation that the goods or services will perform as promised in the agreement; a guaranty. For example, a license agreement relating to a database of samples of musical compositions may contain a warranty that the licensor has obtained permission from the composers and performers of the musical works to provide access to that database to the licensee.

workstation a single terminal or personal computer that may or may not be connected to a larger network.

RESOURCES

The following is a selected list of resources for further reading on licensing electronic content for librarians.

Web Resources

Yale University Library Liblicense, Licensing Digital Information, is an excellent source. It provides descriptions of licensing terms, sample licenses, license vocabulary, various links to other resources, and a place to sign up for one of the best electronic discussion lists in this area, the Liblicense-L Discussion List, at http://www.library.yale.edu/~llicense/.

The University of Texas has a variety of information on copyright and intellectual property. Some interesting items to look at include its Software and Database License Agreement Checklist. See http://www.utsystem.edu/OGC/intellectualproperty.

The EBLIDA (European Bureau of Library, Information and Documentation Associations) site is more focused on Europe, but it has some very helpful information and links on licensing in general, including consortia. See http://www.eblida.org.

Stanford University has helpful information on copyright law and fair use at http://fairuse.stanford.edu/.

The Association of Research Libraries has various sources on digital licensing for libraries, including its document *Licensing Electronic Resources*. See http://www.arl.org/scomm/licensing/.

Columbia University Libraries has a relatively short three-part checklist for a license agreement. See http://www.columbia.edu/cu/libraries/inside/ner/license-checklist.html.

The New England Law Library Consortium, a consortium of twenty-five institutions, has a checklist/worksheet for electronic acquisitions. See http://www.nellco.org/general/criteria.htm.

The University of California Libraries has a document that may help libraries developing their own licensing policies. See http://sunsite.berkeley.edu/Info/ principles.html.

The Association of Learned and Professional Society Publishers has various documents, including a link to the article *Guidelines for Licence of Electronic Publications,* which is a checklist for licensing. See http://www.alpsp.org/ licensing.htm.

Model Licenses

The Liblicense Standard Licensing Agreement was developed for academic libraries but is useful for all library licensing situations. See http://www. library.yale.edu/~llicense/standlicagree.html.

The Licensing Models developed by John Cox consist of four models, one for academic institutions, one for academic consortia, one for public libraries, and one for corporate, government, and other research libraries. See http://www. licensingmodels.com.

The National Electronic Site Licence Initiative (http://www.nesli.ac.uk/nesli8a.html) provides a license based on a draft model agreement by the Joint Information Systems Committee and Publishers Association (www.ukoln.ac.uk/services/elib/papers/pa/licence/ Pajisc21.html).

Licensing Principles

The International Federation of Library Associations and Institutions approved a set of licensing principles for libraries in March 2001 which is available at http://www.ifla.org/V/ebpb/copy.htm.

The Association of Research Libraries published a booklet entitled *Licensing Electronic Resources* in 1997 which sets out various principles and issues relevant to licensing by libraries. It is available at http://www.arl.org/scomm/ licensing/licbooklet.html.

Electronic Discussion Lists

See the Yale University Library LibLicense under "Web Resources."

CNI-Copyright is an open, public electronic forum for discussion of a broad range of copyright and intellectual property-related issues. To subscribe, send a message to listproc@arl.org. The text of the message should read: subscribe cni-copyright [your name].

Collective Societies

The site of the International Federation of Reproduction Rights Organisations provides general information on reprography collectives and some general copyright information, as well as a useful newsletter. The site also has links to reprography collectives in countries around the world. See http://www.ifrro.org.

The U.S.-based Copyright Clearance Center is at http://www.copyright.com.

CANCOPY, which deals with English-language print materials in Canada, is at http://www.cancopy.com.

COPIBEC, which is concerned with French-language print materials in Canada, is at http://www.copibec.qc.ca.

(For more information on these organizations, see the section "Collective Societies and Digital Licensing" in chapter 1 of this book.)

Print Books

Bielefield, Arlene, and Lawrence Cheeseman. *Interpreting and Negotiating Licensing Agreements: A Guidebook for the Library, Research and Teaching Professions*. New York: Neal-Schuman, 1999. This book provides a good general introduction to the area of licensing.

Fisher, Roger, and William Ury. *Getting to Yes: Negotiating Agreement without Giving In*. Toronto: Penguin, 1981. This is a print "classic" for negotiating in general. Many librarians who are involved in license negotiations find this book useful.

INDEX

Lesley Ellen Harris is a lawyer and consultant who works on copyright, licensing, and e-commerce issues in the publishing, entertainment, Internet, and information industries. She began her career in copyright in 1984 working with a lobbying group interested in revising Canada's copyright laws. From 1987 to 1991 she was senior copyright officer for the Canadian government, in which capacity she helped revise the country's copyright laws. Harris is the author of *Digital Property: Currency of the 21st Century* (1997) and *Canadian Copyright Law* (3rd ed., 2001), as well as numerous articles and papers. She maintains the Web site copyrightlaws.com and is editor of *The Copyright and New Media Law Newsletter: For Libraries, Archives and Museums*. She may be reached at libraries@copyrightlaws. com.